Mathematical Word Problems

for Parents to get involved in their child's Maths via word problems

JOHN CARTY

A catalogue record for this book is available from the National Library of Australia

Copyright © 2023 by John Carty

All rights reserved. No part of this book may be reproduced or transmitted in any form or by any means, electronic or mechanical, including photocopying, recording, or by any information storage and retrieval system, without permission in writing from the copyright owner.

Publisher:
Inspiring Publishers
P.O. Box 159, Calwell, ACT Australia 2905
Email: inspiringpublisher.com
http://www.inspiringpublishers.com

National Library of Australia Cataloguing-in-Publication entry

Author: John Carty

Title: **MATHEMATICAL WORD PROBLEMS:**
     for Parents to get involved in their child's Maths via word problems

ISBN: 978-1-923087-72-9 (Print)

Ω
BASIC TYPES

Q1. Mum and Dad bought 3 calculators for $21.40 each. How much change should they get from $100?

Q2. Billy was born in 1956. What age did he turn on his birthday in the year 2015?

MATHEMATICAL WORD PROBLEMS

Q3. The temperature of the element of the stove rises 1 degree celcius per second. How long will it take to rise from 18 degrees celcius to 103 degrees celcius?

Q4. Gerard runs around the park every day. This week his times have been 23 minutes, 26 minutes, 25 minutes and 30 minutes. What has been the average time for his run?

Q5. A cardboard box weighs 250g. It is packed with 6 tins of fruit, each weighing 1.5kg. Calculate the total weight in grams of the packed box.

Q6. A company sent out 9000 reports at a cost of 90 cents each. Find the cost of postage.

Q7. If 4 tickets to the dance costs $26. Find the cost of 10 such tickets.

Q8. A marathon race started at 11.45am and the winner finished at 1.05pm. What was the winner's time?

Q9. Carl is 5 years older than Wendy and Wendy is 8 years older than Diana. If Carl is 3 years younger than Jack, how many years older than Diana is Jack?

Q10. Two angles of a triangle are 37 degrees and 46 degrees. What is the size of the other angle?

Q11. There are 25 people in a class and each of then own a cat or dog or both as pets. If 17 have cats and 14 have dogs, how many have both?

Q12. My cat needs to take 3 tablets each day. How many days will 54 tablets last?

Q13. The area of a square coaster is 64 cm.sq. What is its perimeter?

Q14. A child needs 4ml of medicine twice a day. How many days will a 560ml bottle last?

Q15. A pharmacist packs 36 tablets in each bottle. How many bottles will he use to pack 612 tablets?

Q16. Tommy scored 12 out of 20 for the multi-choice section of his test and 36 out of 60 for the essay part of the same test. What was his overall percentage mark?

Q17. The Hammond family's phone bill is made up of two parts: rental and metered calls. If the rental was $37.85 and the total bill was $93.40. How much did the Hammond family spend on metered calls?

Q18. A train left Gladstone at 11.40pm on a Tuesday night and arrived in Townsville at 10.25am the next day, Wednesday. What was the time for the train's journey?

Q19. How much would an outworker be paid for making 40 shirts, if she is paid $5.50 for each shirt?

BASIC TYPES

Q20. Ray is offered $2.40 per unit to make T-shirts at home. How many will he have to make in order to earn $384?

Q21. The instructions for cooking a frozen dinner indicate it is to be in the oven at 400°C for 22 minutes. Hugh put it in at 7.39pm; when should he take it out?

Q22. Anita bought 4 small chocolates for $2 each and 3 large chocolates for $3 each. How much did she spend?

Q23. My tennis club had $400 in the bank and received sponsorship of $350. We spent $930 in the season. How much are we in debt?

Q24. A farmer had 2500 sheep, but some of them escaped through a broken gate. He then had 1970 sheep. How many escaped?

Q25. Two sisters Nathalia and Diana are 1¾ years apart in age, Nathalia being the older. When Nathalia is 13½ years old, how old will Diana be?

Q26. The school library charges a 3c per day fine for overdue books. Natasha has a Science book 24 days overdue, an English book 6 days overdue and a Commerce book 12 days overdue. If she returns all 3 books today what will be her fine?

Q27. Drina and Mirna have rectangular gardens with the same area. Drina's garden is 24m wide. Mirna's garden is 3m narrower but 10m longer than Drina's. How long is Mirna's garden?

Q28. A school readathon lasted 47 hours. It started at 2pm on Friday. When did it finish?

Q29. The temperature in my lounge room is kept constant at 21°C. Outside it is -13°C. How much warmer is my lounge room than outside?

Q30 Megan withdrew $208.65 from her bank account which had a current balance of $1705.55. What will be her new balance?

Q31. A landslide blocked the railway line at Carrington. It took the train 5 hours to reverse back to Epping at 27km/h. Normally the train travelled at 60km/h. How long normally would it then take to travel back to Carrington?

Q32. A drought in Goulburn caused a water crisis so that its 25000 residents could only use a total of 500 000 litres per day. How much water did this allow each person to have on average?

Q33. Lucy had 45 minutes left to complete an exam. This was 3/8 of the total time. How many minutes of the exam had elapsed (already gone)?

MATHEMATICAL WORD PROBLEMS

Q34. A promoter hired Parramatta Stadium (capacity 24000) for a concert and 13465 people attended. How many seats were empty?

Q35. If Keiran can swim ¾ the way across the pool and Glen can swim 3/10 as far as Keiran, how much of the distance across the pool could Glen swim?

Q36. The local sawmill had a fire that damaged 16% of its stock. Termites ate 1/25 of the stock and a minor flood ruined 2/25 of the stock. What fraction of the total stock is still in good condition?

Q37. The human heart pumps 27000 litres of blood in 24 hours. How many litres of blood is this per hour?

Q38. A carrier from the markets had to deliver 8 crates of rockmelons, with 30 in each crate. It was found that 12 rockmelons were rotten and had to tossed out. What percentage was tossed out?

Q39. A grazier had 3 km of fencing, but a storm blew down one stretch 400m and another stretch twice as long. What fraction of the fence remained?

Q40. There are 10 classes in the local primary school all with the same number of children. If each class was increased by 3 children, there would be one less class (i.e. 9 classes). How many children are in each class?

Q41. In 21 years Gail will be 60 years old. What is her age now?

Q42. Tom weighs 70kg. He has 2 sons, Greg and Brad. Greg weighs 2kgs less than Brad. Together Greg and Brad weigh the same as Tom., What is the weight of each of Tom's sons?

Q43. [Rectangle with top side labelled $2x + 4$ and left side labelled 7]

(a) Write an expression for the area of this rectangle

(b) If the area is 112 square units find the length of the rectangle.

Q44. Two trains leave a station at the same time and travel in the same direction. If train A averages 80 km/h and train B averages 50 km/h, how long will it be before the faster train is 75 km ahead of the slower train?

BASIC TYPES

Q45. Two equilateral triangles of the same size are placed side by side so that they form a parallelogram. If the perimeter of the parallelogram is 96cm, find the length of one side of the equilateral triangle.

Q46. A grazier planted a row of 16 oak trees along the side of his driveway. The trees were planted 4.2 metres apart. What distance along the driveway did the trees stretch?

Q47. A girl sits for a test containing 20 questions. She is awarded 2 marks for each correct answer and 1 mark is subtracted for each incorrect answer. If her final score is 22 marks, how many questions did she have correct?

Q48. How can $200 be invested, one part at 6% and the rest at 4% so that the interest will be the same on each investment.

Q49. Alexander went to sleep at 8.35 p.m. and slept for 8 hours 15 mins. When did he wake up?

Q50 A man drives to the mountains at an average speed of 50 km/h and returns in busy traffic at 40 km/h. If the total travelling time is 9 hours find the distance he travelled to reach the mountains.

Q51. An overseas flight arrived at Brisbane and 96 passengers got off. The plane then flew on to Sydney where the remainder got off. There were 191 passengers originally. How many got off in Sydney?

Q52. The top rung of a ladder is 2.7m above the ground. A man standing on the top rung is 1.92m tall. He wants to touch a ceiling 5m above the floor. How many centimetres above the top of his head must he reach?

Q53. My cycling speed is 8km per hour faster than my walking speed. If I walk for 3 hours and then cycle for 5 hours I will have travelled 88km. What is my walking speed?

Q54. Jessica buys a pen and a ruler for $1.48. Rebecca buys three pens and a ruler for $3.26. What is the cost of the ruler?

Q55. The ages of Mrs Nguyen and her son Luan added together make 51 years. Three years ago Mrs Nguyen was four times as old as Luan. How old is Luan?

Q56. At the Canberra Festival a Round-about ride cost 60c for children and 80c for adults. If 122 tickets are sold on Friday evening giving a total takings of $89.20, how many children went for a ride on the Round-about?

MATHEMATICAL WORD PROBLEMS

Q57. Herb and Rima deliver papers. Between them they deliver a total of 69 papers. If Rima delivers 5 more than Herb, How many papers does Herb deliver?

Q58. A train leaves Brisbane at 8.30pm and arrives in Townsville next morning at 9.15am. How long did the journey take?

Q59. Sarah scored 18 marks more in her Maths test than her German test. Her total for the two was 144; what was her score in German.

Q60. To make a roller-skating rink the cost is $20 per square metre. How much would it cost to make one 40m x 30m?

Q61. Lydia hit her golf ball 3/5 of the way to the green and her sister Maria hit hers ½ way. How much more of the distance from tee to green did Lydia's shot come?

Q62. Thirty staff members ate a banquet meal at a cost of $15 each, but 5 left without paying. How much extra will each of the remaining staff members have to pay to make up for those five?

Q63. A rectangle has sides 7cm and 3cm. Find the length of its diagonals.

Q64. A farmer has a rectangular paddock 350m long and 190m wide.

How much would it cost to fence the paddock at 85 cents per metre?

Q65. A truck is driven out of the Flemington markets carrying 500 boxes each of mass 5.8 kg. When it is driven onto a weighbridge the total mass is 8.1 tonnes. What is the mass of the truck when it is unloaded?

Q66. Determine the length of the second diagonal of a rhombus with sides 7cm and one diagonal 10cm.

Q67. The slant height of a cone is 13cm and its base radius is 5cm. How high is the cone?

Q68. A chord of length 8cm is 4cm from the centre of a circle. Determine the radius of the circle.

Q69. A ship sails 9km due west and then 7km due south. How far is it from its starting point?

Q70. Danica is 8 years older than Monica. The sum of their ages is 38. What is Danica's age?

Q71. Town A is 80km south of town B and town C is 150km east of town B. Is it quicker to travel directly from A to C by car at 90 km/hr or via B by train at 130 km/hr.

BASIC TYPES

Q72. It take 40 L of maple sap to make 1 L of maple syrup. How many litres of maple syrup can be made from 2500 L of maple sap?

Q73. A rectangular box is 2cm x 3cm x 4cm internally. Find the length of the largest toothpick that can be placed within the box.

Q74. It takes me 25 minutes to drive to work. At what time must I leave to reach work 10 minutes early, if I start work at 7.25 am?

Q75. In a year group at school there are 150 pupils, of these 110 study Spanish, 83 study Arabic and 48 study both Spanish and Arabic. How many pupils do not study either of these two languages?

Q76. What is the length, to the nearest cm, of the longest walking stick that can be placed flat in a suitcase 0.4m long and 0.2m wide?

Q77. A farmer puts a fence with 5 strands of wire around a cattle yard. 15 metres of wire remain from a 300 metres roll. Find the perimeter of the yard.

Q78. The cost of 7 pairs of sandals is $76.50 more than the cost of 4 pairs. Find the cost of 1 pair of sandals.

Q79. Maria bought a motor bike at an auction. she had to spend one third as much again to repair it. Her total costs were $5000. How much did she pay for the motor bike at the auction?

Q80. Hugh bought 7 skateboards. Because of the large order, he was given a discount of $15 off the total price of the skateboards. He paid $230 to the salesman. What was the original prise of each skateboard?

Q81. Next year Paul will be twice as old as Francis, and the sum of their ages will be 42. Find their ages today.

Q82. A ribbon is 72 cm long. It is cut into 2 pieces so that one is 1/3 the length of the other. Find the length of the pieces.

Q83. During a school election, 625 votes were cast. Melanie received 75 more votes than Peter. How many votes did Peter receive?

Q84. Peter and Mary have newspaper rounds. Mary's weekly earnings are 3 times Peter's weekly earnings. Together they make $11.00. How much does Mary earn in a week?

Q85. The length of a rectangle, decreased by 1 cm, equals the width of the rectangle. If the perimeter is 102 cm, find the dimensions of the rectangle.

MATHEMATICAL WORD PROBLEMS

Q86. A tiger is awake for twice as long as he is asleep. How long is he asleep for in a day?

Q87. A jogger ran 7 km more on Tuesday than she ran on Monday. If she ran a total of 31 km on these two days, how many kilometres did she run on Monday?

Q88. If 120 passengers each have 50 kg of luggage, what is the total weight in tonnes?

Q89. If 200 grams of sugar are used from a bag containing 2 kg, how many grams of sugar are left?

Q90. A rectangular area 20 m by 15 m is to be sown with grass. If a packet of grass seed covers 5 square metres, how many packets will be needed for this area?

Q.91. A bottle of softdrink weighs 1 kg. If the bottle, when empty, weighs 36 grams, how much does the liquid weigh?

Q92. A television repair man arrived at 11:35 am and finished at 12:20 pm. If he charges $28 an hour, how much will be charged for this service?

Q93. The local garage charges $38 per hour for labour. If your car took 1½ hours to repair, how much would this cost?

Q94.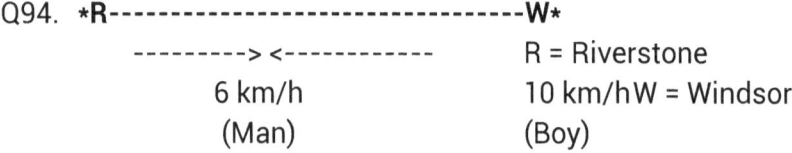

Two towns R and W are 12 kilometres apart. A man sets out to walk from R to W averaging 6km/h. At the same time a boy sets out to run from W to R at an average speed of 10km/h. What time elapses before they meet?

Q95. A racing car uses 22 litres of fuel to travel 440 kms. How far could it travel on 16 litres of fuel?

Q96. A car uses 9.6 litres of petrol to travel 100 km. How many litres of petrol does it need to travel 360 kms?

Q97. A petrol tanker can discharge 430 litres per minute. How long does it take to discharge 3655 litres?

Q98. A shearer in Cootamundra wants to shear an average of 465 sheep per day over the 5 days from Monday to Friday. By Friday he knows he needs to shear 595 sheep on that day to make his average. How many sheep has he shorn on the other 4 days?

BASIC TYPES

Q99. A shearer in Grenfell wants to shear an average of a certain number of sheep per week from Monday to Friday. By the end of Thursday his average is only 440 sheep per day and he will need to shear 640 sheep on Friday to make his average for the week. What was that average?

Q100. A concert consisted of 3 acts of 9 minutes each with a 3 minute break between the first and second act, and a 4 minute break between the second and third act. If the concert finished at 11:04 am, when did it start?

ANSWERS

1. $35.80
2. .59
3. 1 min 25 secs
4. 26 mins
5. 9250 gm
6. $8100
7. $65
8. 1 hr 20 mins
9. 16
10. 97°
11. 6
12. 18
13. 32cm
14. 70
15. 17
16. 60%
17. $55.55
18. 10 hrs 45 mins
19. $220
20. 160
21. 8.01pm
22. $17
23. $180
24. 530
25. 11 3/4
26. $1.26
27. 80 m
28. 1 pm Sunday
29. 34°C
30. $1496.90
31. 2 1/4 hours
32. 20 litres
33. 75 mins
34. 10 535
35. 9/40
36. 18/25
37. 1 125 litres
38. 5%
39. 3/5
40. 27
41. 39
42. Greg - 34 kgs
    Brad - 36 kgs
43. a) A = 14x + 28
    b) 16 units
44. 2 1/2 hours
45. 24 cm
46. 63 metres
47. 14

48. $80 at 6%
    $120 at 4%
49. 4:50 am
50. 200 km
51. 95
52. 38
53. 6 km/h
54. 59c
55. 12 years
56. 42
57. 32
58. 12 hrs 45 mins
59. 63
60. $24000
61. 1/10
62. $3 each
63. $\sqrt{58}$ cm
64. $918
65. 5.2 tonne
66. $2\sqrt{24}$ cm or 9.8cm
67. 12 cm
68. $\sqrt{32}$ cm
69. $\sqrt{130}$ km
70. 23
71. via B is quicker
72. 62.5 L
73. $\sqrt{29}$ cm
74. 6.50 am

75. 5
76. 45 cms
77. 57 m
78. $25.50
79. $3750
80. $35
81. Paul - 27
    Francis - 13
82. 18 cm and 54 cm
83. 275
84. $8.25
85. 25 cm x 26 cm
86. 8 hours
87. 12 km
88. 6 tonnes
89. 1800 gms
90. 60 packets
91. 964 gms
92. $21
93. $57
94. 3/4 hour
95. 320 kms
96. 34.56 L
97. 8.5 minutes
98. 1730
99. 480
100. 10:30 am

Ω
SIMPLE LINEAR EQUATIONS

Q1. The longer side of a rectangular field is 2 1/2 times the shorter side.

The perimeter of the field is 448 metres. What is the length of the longer side?

Q2. A cricket ball costs $6 more than a golf ball. Four cricket balls and three golf balls cost $45. What is the cost of a golf ball?

Q3. A computer cost $450 more than a microwave. Together they cost $2070. What is the cost of the microwave?

SIMPLE LINEAR EQUATIONS

Q4. The jogger Joe runs 3 times as far as he walks. He then rides a bike for 7 km. If he travels 37 km altogether, how far does he walk?

Q5. A CD player costs $77 less than a camcorder. Together they cost $593. How much does the CD player cost?

Q6. One third of a number plus 16 gives 2 times the number minus 4. What is the number?

Q7. The sum of 2 consecutive integers is 23. What are they?

Q8. The sum of 3 consecutive integers is 21. What is the smallest integer?

Q9. Divide $225 between Michael and Joanna so that Michael gets $25 more than Joanna.

Q10. To pay a bill of $125 I use five and ten dollar notes, with half as many of the former as the latter. How many of the five dollar notes do I use?

Q11. A rectangular paddock has a perimeter of 150 m, and its length is 4 times its breadth. What is its length?

Q12. Dad spent $120 buying a present for Mum and their daughter Caroline. If Caroline's present cost 2/3 as much as Mum's present, find the cost of Mum's present.

Q13. A man is now 5 times as old as his son. In 8 years' time he will only be 3 times as old as his son. How old is the father now?

Q14. A motorist drives at a certain speed for 4 hours and then drives for 1/2 hour with his speed increased by 10 km/h. If in this time he travelled 275 km, at what speed did he travel first?

Q15. The sum of 3 numbers is 27. The smallest is half the largest, and the third number is 3 more than the smallest. Find the numbers.

Q16. Pablo has $3 more in his pocket than Danny. Together they have $11. How much has Danny got?

Q17. Con tries to guess the number of lollies in a bottle but guesses 75 too many. Effie tries and guesses 63 too few. The average of their guesses is 350. How many beans are in the bottle?

Q18. Mr Binos is 5 times as old as his son and was 36 years old when his son was bon. How old is Mr Binos?

MATHEMATICAL WORD PROBLEMS

Q19. On an overseas tennis tour Pat has won 50 out of 75 matches played. There are still 45 matches left to play. He wants to win at least 3/5 of all matches on the tour. How many of the remaining 45 must he win?

Q20. Twice a certain number is 14. What is the number?

Q21. Three times a certain number is 27. What is the number?

Q22. Half of a certain number is 8. What is the number?

Q23. One quarter of a certain number is 5. What is the number?

Q24. The length of a rectangular field is 200m greater than its width. If the perimeter is 960m find the width.

Q25. Emily's age in 8 years time is 4/5 of what it will be in 20 years time. What is Emily's age?

Q26. Last weekend Karla earned 3 times as much as Kellie. Together they earned $96. How much did Karla earn?

Q27. The number of pages in one book is 60 more than 5 times the number of pages in another. If together they have 300 pages, how many pages are in each book?

Q28. Three times a certain number is equal to 5 more than twice the number. What is the number:

Q29. If I add 5 to a number and double the result my answer is 14. What is the number?

Q30. If I add 7 to a number and multiply the result by 3, my answer is 27. What is the number?

Q31. If I subtract one from a number and multiply the result by 2, my answer is 20. Find the number.

Q32. If I subtract 8 from a number and multiply the result by 5, the answer is 80. Find the number.

Q33. The perimeter of a square is 20cm. What is the length of each side of the square?

Q34. The perimeter of a square is 72 cm. Find the length of the sides of the square?

Q35. Find the length of the sides of an equilateral triangle whose perimeter is 18 cm.

Q36. Find the length of the sides of an equilateral triangle whose perimeter is 96 cm.

Q37. Carl is 8 years older than Kylie. In 10 years time the sum of their ages will be 48. How old is Carl?

SIMPLE LINEAR EQUATIONS

Q38. Alan picks 50% more peaches than Jimmy. One day they picked 225 cans of peaches between them. How many cans did Alan pick?

Q39. My mother is twice as old as I am. If the sum of our ages is 66, what is my age?

Q40. My examination mark in Mathematics was 20 greater than my French mark. If I scored a total of 170 on the two examinations, what was my mark in each subject?

Q41. The sum of two consecutive numbers is 13. What are the numbers?

Q42. Carlos is twice as old as Angela. Four years ago he was three times as old as Angela. What is Angela's current age?

Q43. The green grocer returned from the markets with 2 large containers of rockmelons. A quarter of the first container were rotten. The second container had one more rockmelon than the first, and only 1/5 of the second container were rotten. In total the green grocer had a total of 69 good rockmelons. How many bad ones were there?

Q44. Two numbers differ by 12. Find the numbers if their sum is 132.

Q45. The sum of 3 consecutive integers is 147. What are the numbers?

Q46. The sum of two numbers is 80. Find the numbers if the greater exceeds twice the lesser by 35.

Q47. The sum of 3 consecutive even integers is 150. What are the numbers?

Q48. The greater of two numbers is equal to 3 times the lesser. Find the numbers if the smaller number, increased by 5, equals the greater number decreased by 45.

Q49. A team scored 30 points in the 2 games they played. In the first game they scored 6 more points than twice the number of points scored in the second game. How many points were scored in each game?

Q50. Two books have a total of 300 pages. However, the number of pages in one book is 60 more than 3 times the number of pages in the other. How many pages are there in each book?

Q51. In a box there are 20 more 5 cent pieces than 10 cent pieces. If the sum of money is $8.50, how many of each coin is there?

Q52. Cindy invested two amounts of money that differed by $80. The greater part was invested at 6% p.a and the other at 10% p.a. If the total interest earned was $24, how much money was invested at each rate?

MATHEMATICAL WORD PROBLEMS

Q53. During last year the Raiders lost 3 times as many games as they won. They also tied 2 fewer games than they won. If the season had 18 games, how many games were won? How many were lost?

Q54. Last season the Lakers won twice as many games as they lost, but tied 7 games less than they won. If they played a total of 23 games, they how many did they win?

Q55. Each ham is placed in a plastic casing to protect and seal the flavour. In each box 12 hams are then packed. If in a certain shipment 2 fewer hams were packed in each box, then 8 more boxes would be needed. How many hams were in the original shipment?

Q56. The rectangular backyard has a perimeter of 112m. If the length is 24m longer than the width, find its dimensions.

Q57. The length of a box when decreased by 6cm is equal to the width. If the perimeter is 68cm, find its dimensions.

Q58. The width and length of a rectangular gym floor differ by 6m. If the perimeter of the floor is 76m, find its area.

Q59, The length of a rectangular room is 2m greater than twice the width. If the perimeter of the room is 34m, what is the area?

Q60. At the school concert, 209 tickets were sold. If there were 23 more student tickets sold than twice the number of adult tickets, how many of each were sold?

Q61. A team scored 102 points in their first 3 games. In the first game they scored twice as many points as in the second game. In the last game they scored 8 points less than the first game. How many points were scored in each game?

Q62. Helen has $300 more than twice what Mary has. If they have $1500 in all, how much does each person have?

Q63. How would you divide $33 000 among 3 people so that the first person has twice as much money as the second person and has three times as much money as the third person?

Q64. Last year $2750 was awarded in scholarships to Abdul, Moe and Cass. If Cass received 3 times what Abdul received, and Moe received $250 more than Abdul how much did each of them receive?

Q65. When 14 is added to five times a certain number, the result is 4. Find the number.

SIMPLE LINEAR EQUATIONS

Q66. If 7 is subtracted from one third of a certain number, the result is - 9. Find the number.

Q67. The length of a certain rectangle can be found by tripling the width and adding 4. If the perimeter of the rectangle is 144m, find its dimensions.

Q68. When 3 is added to a certain number and the result is divided by 2, the answer is ½. What is the number?

Q69. Roger is presently 12 years older than Tim. In 10 years time, twice Roger's age will be equal to 3 times Tim's age. How old are they today?

Q70. If 12 is subtracted from 4 times a certain number and the result is multiplied by 3, the answer is 12. What is the number?

Q71. When 4 times a certain fraction is subtracted from 8, the result is 2. Find the fraction.

Q72. The sum of two consecutive numbers is 35. What is the larger number?

Q73. The sum of three consecutive numbers is 72. Find the numbers.

Q74. The sum of three consecutive *even* numbers is 312. What are the numbers?

Q75. If the sum of four consecutive *odd* numbers is 72, find the smallest number.

Q76. The sides of a quadrilateral have lengths which are consecutive whole numbers. If the perimeter is 42 metres, determine the length of the shortest side.

Q77. Farmer Diaz required 560 metres of fencing to enclose a rectangular paddock. If the length is 40 metres longer than the width, calculate the dimensions of the paddock.

Q78. On one particular pay day when Peta collects her pay cheque, she is pleasantly surprised. On top of her normal fortnightly pay, she also receives a bonus equal to one-eighth of her normal fortnightly pay, an award equal to three times her normal fortnightly pay, and a holiday loading equal to three-quarters of her fortnightly pay. Peta notices that if she divides her pay cheque by 130, the result just happens to be her favourite number which is 24. Calculate her normal fortnightly pay.

Q79. A beaker of liquid is at a temperature of 12° and is heated up 8 °C every minute. Write a formula to express the temperature, t, of the liquid after m minutes. If another beaker containing a different liquid at 22 °C is heated at the same time at a rate of 7 °C every minute calculate the amount of time taken for the two beakers to reach the same temperature. What is this temperature and how long did it take to reach this temperature?

MATHEMATICAL WORD PROBLEMS

Q80. A taxi fare is made up of a flag fall and a charge per kilometre travelled. Mrs Cortez was driven 7 km to the station for a cost of $8.10 and 12 km back from the shopping centre at a cost of $12.10. Find the flagfall and the cost per kilometre.

Q81. Hilary has $3.90 which is just enough money to buy 6 apples and 9 bananas. However, if she bought 4 apples and 11 bananas she would have 10c left. Calculate the cost each of an apple and a banana.

Q82. A ticket for a model train display costs $3 for adults and $1 for children. If 96 tickets were sold for a total day's takings of $180, how many adult tickets and how many children's tickets were sold?

Q83. An amusement ground ride has a short ride for 70c and a long ride for $1.10. If 42 people paid a total of $36.20 for rides, how many people took the short ride?

Q84. A two digit number is four times the sum of its digits. If the digits are reversed, the new number is 27 more than the original number. Find the number.

Q85. A two digit number is 7 times the sum of its digits. If the digits are reversed, the new number is 18 less than the original number. Find the number.

Q86. Two numbers are such that if 3/4 of the bigger is added to ½ of the smaller, the result is 14. If 1/5 of the smaller is subtracted form 2/3 of the bigger, the result is 6. Find the numbers.

Q87. A station is 1.8 kilometres away. I walk at 6 kilometres an hour then run at 10 kilometres per hour, reaching the station in 14 minutes. How far did I walk?

Q88. In a factory the fitters earn $30 per day, and the trainees $18 per day. 150 people earn $3 660.00 a day How many fitters are there?

Q89. A school buys 5 gross of pencils for $15.57. Some are bought at $1.60 and the rest $2.50, per hundred. How many of the first kind were bought? N.B a gross is 144.

Q90. The length of a certain rectangle can be found by doubling the width and subtracting 3m. Find its dimensions if the perimeter is 84m.

Q91. A certain number is added to both the numerator and the denominator of the fraction 11/29 to form a new fraction 4/7. What number is added to each?

Q92. To change Celsius temperatures to Fahrenheit temperatures the formula $F = 9C/5 + 32$ is used. What is the temperature which has the same number of degrees on both scales?

SIMPLE LINEAR EQUATIONS

Q93. In an examination one-third of the candidates fail. In the next examination one-quarter of the candidates fail. If there were 24 more candidates and 32 fewer failures in the second examination, how many candidates were there at the first examination?

Q94. A newspaper boy buys 18 dozen papers at 96c per dozen. He sells some at $1.20 per dozen. He returns the rest and receives 72c per dozen. He makes $3.60 profit. How many does he sell?

Q95. The sum of the interior angles of a polygon of n sides is given by the formula $S = (2n - 4)$ right angles. Find the number of degrees in each interior angle of a regular 9 - sided figure. Find also the number of sides if each interior angle is $162°$.

Q96. Roger cycles 10 km at a certain speed, then motors 50km at 3 times that speed. Altogether he is travelling 1 hour 20 minutes. Find his cycling speed.

Q97. The sum of two whole numbers is 15 and their difference is 1. Find the numbers.

Q98. The sum of two whole numbers is 8 and their difference is 12. Find the numbers.

Q99. The sum of two whole numbers is 7. Twice the larger less the smaller is 5. Find the two numbers.

Q100. Find two numbers such that twice the larger plus the smaller is 0 and three times the larger less the smaller is 5.

Q101. The length of a rectangle is 2cm more than the width. If the perimeter of the rectangle is 68 cm, find the length and the width.

Q102. One small bar of chocolate and one ice cream cost 48c whilst two similar bars of chocolate and one ice cream cost 76c. Find the cost of the chocolate and the ice cream.•

Q103. In the examinations a student's Maths mark exceeded her English mark by 21. If the total marks gained in the two examinations was 137, find her mark in each subject.

Q104. My French mark is 15 less than my Maths mark and the total of my two marks is 145. Find my two marks.

Q105. To the double of a certain number I add 14 and obtain 154 as a result. What is the number?

Q106. By adding 46 to a certain number I obtain as a result a number three times as large as the original number. Find the original number.

MATHEMATICAL WORD PROBLEMS

Q107. Divide 84 into two parts so that three times one part is equal to four times the other.

Q108. Alan is twice as old as Bridget and 22 years ago he was three times as old as Bridget was. What is Alan's age?

Q109. Amy is three times as old as Brad and 19 years hence she will be only twice as old as Brad. What is the age of each?

Q110. Find three consecutive numbers whose sum is 45.

Q111. Find five consecutive odd numbers whose sum is 35.

Q112. Two children have $84 together and one has 6 times as much as the other. How much has each?

Q113. A bag contains 35 coins. Some are 10 cent and the rest are 20 cent coins and together they amount to $4. How many of each are there?

Q114. There are 360 people at a concert; some paid $1 and a the rest paid $2; the takings were $520. How many paid $1?

Q115. David completes a journey from Penrith to Blaxland at a certain uniform speed in 5 hours. If on the return journey he travels at half the speed he finds that after 8 hours he has still 3 km to go. Find his original speed.

Q116. Alan and Bridget divide a sum of $70 between them so that Bridget has $10 more than Alan. How much has each?

Q117. Find two numbers whose difference is 14 and sum is 48.

Q118. A tank partly filled with water was completely filled by pouring in 42 litres more and there was then 7 times as much in the tank as before. What was the capacity of the tank in litres?

Q119 Silk costs twice as much as linen and thirty metres of silk and forty metres of linen cost $250. Find the cost of a metre of each.

Q120. Three persons Alan, Brian and Chris have $80 between them. Brian has $20 more than Alan and Chris has as much as Alan and Brian together. How much has each?

Q121. Divide $750 between Alan, Brian and Chris so that Alan has $50 less than Brian and Brian has $50 less than Chris.

Q122. A father is 34 and his son is 4 years old. In how many years will the age of the father be just twice that of the son?

SIMPLE LINEAR EQUATIONS

Q123. A horse costs twice as much as a cow; also 6 horses and 10 cows cost $2,200. Find the price of each horse and cow.

Q124. Mick bought a second-hand motor car and gained one-fifth of what he paid for it by selling it for $1,200. How much did he pay for it?

Q125. Tickets at a school disco cost $1.20 for students and $1.50 for visitors. In all 270 tickets were sold and $358.50 was collected. How many visitors attended?

Q126. Divide 20 into two parts so that if three times one part is added to five times the other part the sum may be 84.

Q127. Alan is twice as old as Bridget and 20 years ago he was three times as old as Bridget. What is the age of each?

Q128. Simon, who walks 9 km each day, sets out from Goulburn, which is 204 km from Sydney, to walk to Sydney. At the same time, Kerry who cycles 25 km per day, sets out from Sydney to ride to Goulburn. In how many days will they meet?

Q129. A bill of $60 is paid with $5 notes and $1 notes. There were 7 times as many $1 as $5 notes. How many notes of each kind were there?

Q130. A casting, weighing 156 kg is made of an alloy of copper and zinc in the ration of 8 parts of copper to every 5 parts of zinc. What weight of each metal was used?

Q131. A farmer has a certain number of cattle worth $18 each and twice as many sheep worth $3.50 each; if their total value is $500, how many has he of each?

Q132. A rectangle has its sides in the ratio of 7 is to 3. If the area of the rectangle is 336 square metres, find the perimeter.

Q133. $640 is distributed between 3 persons A, B and C so that B's share is three-fifths of A's and C's share is equal to the combined shares of A and B. How much does each receive?

Q134. The base of an isosceles triangle is 22 cm and its perimeter is 90 cm. Find the length of each of the equal sides.

Q135. The sum of the angles of any triangle is 180°. One angle of a triangle is twice as large as another angle of the triangle. The third angle is equal to twice the sum of the first two. Find the size of each angle of the triangle.

Q136. A lady is four times as old as her son, and her daughter is 5 years younger than her brother. If their ages add to 79 years, what is the age of the mother?

MATHEMATICAL WORD PROBLEMS

Q137. In a roll of notes there are four times as many $20 notes as $10 notes. If the total sum is $1080 and the notes are all either tens or twenties, how many of each kind are there?

Q138. A swimming pool can be filled by either of two pipes of different size diameters. If the larger pipe alone is used, the pool can be filled in 3 hours. The smaller pipe alone can fill it in 5 hours. Find the time required if both pipes are used.

Q139. Two girls, each with a bicycle, start towards each other at the same time from two towns 80 km apart. If the first girl travels at 14 km/h, what must be the rate of the second cyclist if they meet in 2½ hours?

Q140. Two steamships start from ports 2580 nautical miles apart and travel toward each other. The speed of the faster vessel is 18 knots more than that of the slower ship. Find their rates in knots if they pass in 30 hours. (A knot is 1 nautical mile per hour.)

Q141. A cyclist averaging 15 km/h sets out for a town 180 kms away. Four hours later a motorcyclist sets out from the town to meet the cyclist. How far from the town will the meeting take place if the motorcycle travels at 60 km/h?

Q142. One stenographer can type a certain manuscript in 4 hours, and a second typist could do it in 10 hours. If they both start on the job, what fraction of it will be completed in 1 hour? How long will it take them to do the entire job?

Q143. The petty cash drawer contained 44 stamps valued at $18.80. Some of them were 40c stamps and the rest were 50c stamps. How many of each were there?

Q144. A moneybox contains $1.55 in 5c and 10c coins. If there are 7 more 5c coins than 10c coins, what is the number of each?

Q145. An audience of 765 people paid a total of $2785.00 to see the school play. If an adult ticket cost $5 and a student ticket cost $3, how many students paid admission.

Q146. I think of a number, double it, and subtract 6. The result is 34. Find the number.

Q147. I add 45 to a certain number and the result is six times the original number. Find the number.

Q148. The length of a rectangle is 6 m greater than the width. The perimeter of the rectangle is 72 m. Find the dimensions of the rectangle.

Q149. I think of a number, divide it by 8 and add 9. The result is 30. Find the number.

Q150. Three times a certain number is 8 more than 34. Find the number.

Q151. Twice a certain number is 8 less than 92. Find the number.

SIMPLE LINEAR EQUATIONS

Q152. By adding a certain number to 12, the result is the same as subtracting the number from 32. Find the number.

Q153. The sum of a number and the next number below it is 13. Find the number.

Q154. The base of an isosceles triangle is 8 cm shorter than the sum of the two equal sides. If the perimeter of the triangle is 80 cm find the length of each side.

Q155. The sum of a number and four times that number is 30. Find the number.

Q156. Four students go on the St Vincent de Paul camp. Two of these spent twice as much time on the camp as the other two. Altogether 192 hours was spent on the camp by the students. How much time did each student spend.

Q157. The sum of three consecutive even numbers is 24. Find the smallest of these.

Q158. A father is 30 years old and his daughter is 1 year old. In how many years will the father be twice as old as his daughter.

Q159. Divide 70 into two parts so that their difference is 20.

Q160. The difference between half of certain number and one-third of it is 17. Find the number.

Q161. Three-quarters of a number added to two-thirds of it is equal to 85. Find the number.

Q162. The sum of three consecutive odd numbers is 51. Find the numbers.

Q163. A certain number of dollars and twelve times as many cents make $12.32. How many dollars are there?

Q164. A certain number of dollars and four times as many 5 cents coins make $15.60. How many dollars are there?

Q165. Divide $316 between Ashley, Bob and Clare so that Bob may have $25 more than Ashley and Clare may have $35 more than Bob.

Q166. There are a certain number of 10 cent and 5 cent coins in a money box. Altogether there is $5.55 in the box and 57 coins. How many 5 cent coins are there?

Q167. From a certain number, 2 is subtracted, the remainder is divided by 5. 5 is added to the quotient and the result is divided by 4, with the final result 3. Find the number.

Q168. The width of a rectangular shed is 3/5 of its length. If the shed had been 6m wider and its length 6 m less, it would have been square. Find the dimensions.

MATHEMATICAL WORD PROBLEMS

Q169. Find two consecutive numbers so that one-sixth of the smaller added to one-fifth of the larger is equal to 9.

Q170. Two numbers differ by 14, and one number is 9/11 of the other. Find the numbers.

Q171. Find two consecutive odd numbers such that one-seventh of the larger exceeds one-ninth of the smaller by 4.

Q172. Three students go on the Salvation Army doorknock. One of these students spent twice as much time as each of the other two. Altogether 22 hours was spent on the doorknock. How much time did each student spend?

Q173. A boy counts three marks for each sum he gets right and subtracts one mark for each sum he gets wrong. He does 20 sums and obtains 32 marks. How many sums did he get right?

Q174. When 6 is subtracted from five times a certain number, the remainder is 69. Find the number.

Q175. A boy is 4 years older than his sister. If the sum of their ages is 28 years, what is the age of each?

Q176. Mary is three times as old as John. The difference in their ages is 14 years. How old is Mary?

Q177. A department store orders 1000 one kilogram bags of candies to cost $6 per bag. If the manufacturer has candies costing $5.50 and $7.50 per kilogram, how many kilograms of each can be put in the mixture?

Q178. A dealer wishes to mix nuts worth $6.40 per kilogram with nuts at $4 per kilogram in order to make a mixture of 160 kilograms of nuts to sell at $5.20 per kilogram. How many kilograms of each should he use in the mixture?

Q179. Perfume is sold in 10 ml and 25 ml bottles. A distributor orders 33 bottles of perfume, receiving a total of 600 ml. How many bottles of each did she receive?

Q180. A distributor has to fill 20 ml and 70 ml bottles of mineral water for marketing purposes. He has 970 ml of mineral water. How many of each type of bottle should he fill if he has 21 bottles in total?

Q181. An orchardist in Renmark sells his oranges in small bags of 8 and large bags of 20. He sorted 560 oranges into 46 bags. How many of each type of bag did he sort?

ANSWERS

1. 160 m
2. $3
3. $810
4. 7.5 km
5. $258
6. 12
7. 11, 12
8. 6
9. $125, $100
10. 5
11. 60 cm
12. $72
13. 40 years
14. 60 km per hour
15. 6, 9, 12
16. $4
17. 344
18. 45
19. 22
20. The number is 7
21. The number is 9
22. The number is 16
23. The number is 20
24. 140m
25. 40 years
26. $72
27. 40, 260
28. The number is 5
29. The number is 2
30. The number is 2
31. The number is 11
32. The number is 24
33. 5cm
34. 18cm
35. 6cm
36. 32cm
37. 18 years
38. 135
39. 22 years
40. *Maths* = 95%, *French* = 75%
41. 6,7
42. 8 years
43. 20
44. 72, 60

MATHEMATICAL WORD PROBLEMS

45. 48, 49, 50
46. 65, 15
47. 48, 50, 52
48. 75, 25
49. 8, 22
50. 240, 60
51. 50 10-cents, 70 5-cents
52. $200 at 6%, $120 at 10%
53. 4 won, 12 lost
54. 12 won
55. 480
56. 40m by 16m
57. 20cm x 14cm
58. 352m²
59. 60m²
60. 147 students 62 adult
61. 44, 22, 36
62. $1100, $400
63. $18 000, $9 000, $6 000
64. Abdul $500, Moe $750, Cass $1500
65. - 2
66. - 6
67. 55m, 17m
68. - 2
69. Roger 26, Tim 14
70. 4
71. 1½
72. 18
73. 23, 24, 25
74. 102, 104, 106
75. 15
76. 9 m
77. 120 m x 160 m
78. $640
79. 92°C, 10 minutes
80. Flagfall - $2.50, 80C per km
81. apple - 29c, banana - 24c
82. 42 adults, 54 children
83. 25
84. 36
85. 42
86. 12, 10
87. 4/5 Kilometre
88. 80
89. 270
90. 27m, 15m
91. 13
92. -40°
93. 456
94. 16½ dozen

SIMPLE LINEAR EQUATIONS

95. 140°, 20
96. 20 km per hour
97. 8, 7
98. 10, −2
99. 4, 3
100. 1, −2
101. $l = 18$ cm, $w = 16$ cm
102. Chocolate 28 cents, Ice-cream 20 cents
103. Maths: 79%, English: 58%
104. French: 65%, Maths: 80%
105. 70
106. 23
107. 48, 36
108. 88 years
109. 57, 19 years
110. 14, 15, 16
111. 3, 5, 7, 9, 11
112. $72, $12
113. 30 10cent coins, 5 20cent coins
114. 200
115. 3 k.p.h.
116. $40, $30
117. 31, 17
118. 49 litres
119. Linen $2.50, Silk $5
120. $10, $30, $40
121. $200, $250, $300
122. 26
123. $200 for each horse, $100 for each cow.
124. $1,000
125. 115 visitors
126. 8, 12
127. 80 yrs, 40 yrs.
128. 6
129. 35 $1 notes, 5 $5 notes
130. 96 kg (copper), 60 kg (zinc)
131. 20 cattle, 40 sheep
132. 80 metres
133. $200, $120, $320
134. 34 cm
135. 20°, 40°, 120°
136. 56 years
137. 12 $10 notes, 48 $20 notes
138. 1 hr 52½ minutes
139. 18 km/h
140. 34 knots and 52 knots
141. 96 km
142. 7/20, 2 h 51 mins
143. 32 @ 40c and 12 @ 50c
144. 8 10c coins and 15 5c coins

MATHEMATICAL WORD PROBLEMS

145. 520
146. 20
147. 9
148. 15 m, 21 m
149. 168
150. 14
151. 42
152. 10
153. 7
154. 22, 22, 36
155. 6
156. 32hr, 32hr, 64hr, 64hr
157. 6
158. 28 years time.
159. 45, 25
160. 102
161. 60
162. 15, 17, 19
163. 11
164. 13
165. Ashley $77, Bob $102, Clare $137
166. 3
167. 37
168. 30 m long 18 m wide
169. 24, 25
170. 63, 77
171. 119, 117
172. 5½ hr, 5½ hr, 11hr
173. 13
174. 15
175. 12 and 16 years
176. 21 years
177. 750 kg @ $5.50, and 250 kg @ $7.50
178. 80 kg of each
179. 15 small (10 ml) bottles and 18 large (25 ml) bottles
180. 10 small bottles and 11 large bottles
181. 30 small bags and 16 large bags

Ω
SIMULTANEOUS EQUATIONS

Q1. A sports club bought 7 golf balls and 8 cricket balls for $77. If it had bought 9 golf balls and 5 cricket balls it would have spent $62. What is the cost of a golf ball and a cricket ball?

Q2. A farmer used 53 kgs of fertiliser on his two crops of sweet corn and beetroot. He had planted 6 hectares of sweet corn and 7 hectares of beetroot. Had he planted 9 hectares of sweet corn and only 4 hectares of beetroot he would have used only 47 kgs of fertiliser. How much fertiliser per hectare does the farmer use on each crop?

MATHEMATICAL WORD PROBLEMS

Q3. A wildlife park has 7 kangaroos and 8 emus and its daily food requirement for these animals is 80 units. If it had 11 kangaroos and 9 emus its daily food requirements would be 115 units. What is the daily food requirements for 1 kangaroo and 1 emu?

Q4. A health promotion unit produced 2 booklets, one on arthritis and one on hearing loss. They produced 300 copies of the arthritis booklet and 500 copies of the hearing loss booklet using a total of 10,800 pages. Had they produced 700 copies of the arthritis booklet and 600 copies of the hearing loss booklet they would have used 18,400 pages. How many pages are in each booklet?

Q5. The sum of two numbers is 49, and their difference is 19. Find the numbers.

Q6. The difference between two numbers is 34. The sum of the same two numbers is 84. Find the numbers.

Q7. When two numbers are added, the result is 121. The difference between the numbers is 43. Find the larger of the two numbers.

Q8. Amos is thinking of two whole numbers. When he multiplies the first number by 3 and adds the second number, he gets 39. The difference between the two numbers is 9. Find the numbers.

Q9. Olga thinks of two whole numbers. If she multiplies the first by 2 and adds the second, she gets 95. The difference between the two numbers is 28. Find the numbers.

Q10. The sum of two numbers is 57, and the greater exceeds three times the smaller by 13. Find the numbers.

Q11. Seven containers of bream and five containers of tuna have a net weight of 145 kgs. Five containers of bream and six containers of tuna weight 140 kgs. If all tuna are the same weight and all bream are the same weight, what is the weight of a container of bream and a container of tuna?

Q12. In order to make 5 pig pens and 4 horse yards, a farmer uses 88 metres of fencing. His neighbour used 116 metres of fencing to construct 4 pig pens and 7 horse yards. What amount of fencing is needed to build one pig pen and one horse yard?

Q13. A carrier used 67 m of rope to fasten 3 crates of oranges and 7 crates of pumpkins at the markets. Had he fastened 8 crates of oranges and 6 crates of pumpkins, he would have used 90 m of rope. How much rope is needed to fasten a crate of oranges?

SIMULTANEOUS EQUATIONS

Q14. Seven staff and five students pay $174 a week for parking; eight staff and nine students pay $235 a week for parking. What would ten staff and seven students pay for parking in a week?

Q15. At the market you can buy kiwi fruit in large or small boxes. If you buy 8 large and 5 small boxes you will get 121 kiwi fruit in total. If you buy 3 large and 7 small boxes you will get 71 kiwi fruit in total. How many kiwi fruit are in a large box?

Q16. If I walk for 4 hours and cycle for 3 hours, I travel 76 km. If I walk 6 hours and cycle for 2.5 hours, I travel 78 km. Find my walking speed assuming both are constant.

Q17. The perimeter of a rectangle is 64 metres. Its length is 6 meters greater than its breadth. Find its length and its area.

Q18. If 12,000 adults and 2,000 children pay $6,400 to see a football match, while 9,000 adults and 2,500 children pay $5,000. Find the charges for admission for an adult and for a child.

Q19. On a boat trip, a man goes for 3 hours at one speed and 4 hours at another speed, travelling 265 km altogether. On the return trip (also of 265 km), he travels 5 hours at the first speed and for 2¼ hours at the second speed. Find the two speeds.

Q20. If 24 envelopes and 18 stamps cost $41.70; 16 envelopes and 11 stamps cost $26.55. Find the cost of a envelopes and a stamps.

Q21. The charge for 15 persons for a cookie each and 12 for a coffee is $48. The charge for 12 persons for a cookie each and 16 for a coffee is $54.40. Find the charge for each person for a cookie and a coffee.

Q22. Suppose 12 cases of apples and 7 cases of oranges cost $102; and 7 cases of apples and 9 cases of oranges cost $89. Find the cost of a case of each.

Q23. The difference between the cost of 10 cars and 7 motor cycles is $35,050. The difference between the cost of 7 cars and 10 motor cycles is $20,200. Find the cost of each car and each motor cycle.

Q24. One-third of the sum of two numbers is 14. One half of their difference is 5. Find the numbers.

Q25. Half the sum of two whole numbers is 23, and twice their difference is 24. Find the numbers.

MATHEMATICAL WORD PROBLEMS

Q26. Six horses and seven cows can be bought for $5000. Eleven horses and thirteen cows cost $9,220. Find the cost of each animal.

Q27. Half a dozen eggs and half a dozen bananas cost $4.80. One dozen eggs and 4 bananas cost $7.20. What is the price of each?

Q28. An amount of $80 was paid to a bank teller in 10 dollar notes and 2 dollar notes. There were 12 notes in all. How many notes of each denomination were there?

Q29. Sandra has twice as much money as Sue. If I give Sue $1.25 she will have three times as much as Sandra. How much has Sandra?

Q30. A purse contains only 10¢ pieces and 5¢ pieces to the value of $1. Twice as many 10¢ coins and three times as many 5¢ coins would total $2.40. How many 5¢ coins are in the purse?

Q31. Jack is six years older than Bill. In three years time, Jack will be twice as old as Bill. How old is Bill now?

Q32. Two numbers are such that twice the first added to the second gives 18, whilst twice the first added to twice the second gives 16. Find the numbers.

Q33. Find two positive numbers which differ by 18 and the larger one is two and a half times the smaller one.

Q34. One number is ten less than another, but the larger number added to three times the smaller number gives 34. Find the two numbers.

Q35. Two numbers differ by 5, but twice the smaller number added to the larger number is 14. Find the numbers.

Q36. Twice the length plus twice the width of a rectangle (i.e. the perimeter) totals 14 cm, but the difference between the length and the width is 3 cm. Find the length and the width.

Q37. Five icy poles and three cans of drink cost $14.50, while 2 icy poles and three cans of drink cost $11.20. What is the cost of an icy pole and of a drink?

Q38. The charge for 4 persons for breakfast is $10, and the charge for 6 persons for breakfast and dinner is $51. What is the cost of one person for breakfast? What is the cost of one person for dinner?

Q39. One cricket bat and 6 balls cost $80, while another order of one bat and 9 balls cost $95. What is the cost of a bat and of a ball?

SIMULTANEOUS EQUATIONS

Q40. Two shirts and a pair of gloves cost $29, while three pairs of gloves and 3 shirts cost $66. What is the cost of a shirt, and of a pair of gloves?

Q41. A father's age minus three times his daughter's age gives zero. The sum of their ages is 52 years. Find the age of each.

Q42. Seven adult concert tickets and five children's tickets cost $25, while 2 adult's and 5 children's tickets cost $12.50. Find the cost of an adult's ticket and of a child's ticket.

Q43. Two numbers are such that if 19 is added to the first, the result is twice the second number and if 1 is added to the second number the result is twice the first number. Find the numbers.

Q44. If 3 apples and 4 oranges cost 51 cents while 5 apples and 3 oranges cost 63 cents. Find the cost of an apple and an orange.

Q45. The cost of cleaning 2 sports jackets is the same as the cost of cleaning 5 pairs of trousers. If a jacket and a pair of trousers together cost $21 to clean, find the cost of cleaning each.

Q46. If Rodney gives Jennifer $3 they will both have the same amount. How much does each have if together they have $12.

Q47. The number of one cent coins in a money box is 2 less than 3 times the number of five cent coins. If the total value of the coins is $1.50, how many one cent coins are there.

Q48. A purse contains 34 coins, all of 10 cents or 5 cents. The total value of the coins is $2.85, how many 10 cents coins are there?

Q49. A motorist travels from Goulburn to Dubbo, a distance of 410 kms, the journey taking 9 hours. For part of the time he averaged 50 km/h, and for the rest of the time 40 km/h. How long did he travel at 40 km/h? How far did he travel at 50 km/h?

Q50. How many kg of tea worth 65¢ a kg must be mixed with tea worth 73¢ a kg to give 12 kg of tea each worth 71¢ a kg?

Q51. Find a fraction which becomes 2/3 (two-thirds) when its numerator is doubled and 5 is added to its denominator, and becomes ¾ when its denominator is doubled and 3 is added to its numerator.

Q52. A man plants 1050 shrubs in rows. Some rows contain 45 plants and others 40. There are 3 times as many rows which contain 45 as those which contain 40. How many rows contain 45?

MATHEMATICAL WORD PROBLEMS

Q53. ABC is a triangle whose perimeter is 24 m. Find the length of each side if AC + BC = 2AB and AB + AC = 3BC.

Q54. A cabinet maker has 13 table tops and 45 table legs. He can made 4-legged tables and 3-legged tables. If he uses all of the materials available, how many tables of each type does he make?

Q55. A coin counting machine can record the number of coins counted and their total value. On a particular day it counted 20¢ and 50¢ coins only, and in counting 2070 coins, it noted their total value was $600. How many of each type of coin was counted?

Q56. If 3 packets of bubble gum and 2 chocolates cost 70¢; and 6 packets of bubble gum and 5 chocolates cost $1.60. Find the cost in cents of 1 packet of bubble gum and each bar of chocolate.

Q57. Two farmers buy cows and sheep at a sale yard. 3 cows and 5 sheep cost one farmer $450. The other bought 4 cows and 10 sheep for $700. Find the cost of each cow and each sheep.

Q58. Suppose 2 pairs of gloves and 3 shirts cost $76; and that 7 pairs of gloves and 9 shirts cost $248. Find the cost of each pair of gloves and each shirt.

Q59. Tickets for a school play are 40¢ for adults and 10¢ for children. Altogether 550 people attended. The amount of money collected was exactly $100. How many adults attended? How many children attended?

Q60. In a farmyard, there was a group of cows and hens. The number of legs was 84 more than twice the number of heads. How many cows were there?

Q61. The sum of two natural numbers is 90 and the larger of the two numbers is the square of the smaller. Find the numbers.

Q62. If the difference between two natural numbers is 91 and the larger number is twice the square of the smaller, find the two numbers.

Q63. If the length of a rectangle is half the square of its breadth and its perimeter is 24 cm, find the dimensions of the rectangle.

Q 64. If the length of a rectangle is one quarter of the square of its breadth and its perimeter is 30 cm, find the dimensions of the rectangle.

Q65. If the difference between two natural numbers is 29 and the larger number is one less than the square of the smaller, find the two numbers.

SIMULTANEOUS EQUATIONS

Q66. The sum of two natural numbers is 43. If the larger number is three more than half the square of the smaller, find the numbers.

Q67. A polygon of n sides has $\frac{n}{2}(n-3)$ diagonals. If a polygon has 25 fewer sides than diagonals, find the number of sides and numbers of diagonals.

Q68. A polygon has three more diagonals than sides. Use the formula given in question 67 to find the number of sides and number of diagonals.

Q69. The sum of the n intergers is $S = \frac{n}{2}(n+1)$. If the sum of n intergers is 60 more than 10 times the number of intergers, find the sum of the intergers.

Q70. Half the sum of two numbers is 20 and three times their difference is 30. Find the numbers.

Q71. If one of two numbers be multiplied by 3 and the other by 4, the sum of the products is 43; and if the former be multiplied by 7 and the latter by 3, the difference between these results is 14. Find the numbers.

Q72. A certain fraction becomes 2 when 7 is added to its numerator but becomes unity when 1 is subtracted from its denominator. What is the fraction?

Q73. Four times Bob's age exceeds Alice's age by twenty years and one third of Alice's age is less than Bob's age by two years. Find their ages.

Q74. A man's age is ten times that of his son and in six years time it will be four times that of his son. Find their present ages.

Q75. A certain fraction becomes ½ when 7 is added to its denominator and 2 when 13 is added to its numerator. Find the fraction.

Q76. The sum of two numbers is 33. Their difference is 9. Find the numbers.

Q77. The sum of two numbers is 16. Their difference is 7. Find the numbers.

Q78. The larger of two whole numbers is 4 times the smaller. If the sum of the two numbers is 65, find the numbers.

Q79. Two writing pads and one packet of envelopes cost 61¢. Three pads and three packets of envelopes cost $1.14. Find the cost of each article.

Q80. One orange and five bananas cost $2. Four oranges and nine bananas cost $4.70. What was the cost of each piece of fruit?

MATHEMATICAL WORD PROBLEMS

Q81. Two equal angles of an isosceles triangle are $(2x + y)°$ and $(3x - 2y)°$. The other angle is 40°. Find the values of x and y.

Q82. School photographs are sold in such a way that 4 single and 3 group photographs cost $33, and 5 single and 2 group photographs cost $29. What is the cost of a group photograph?

Q83. An emu farm sell emu eggs in large and small boxes. Five small boxes and 4 large boxes contain 79 emu eggs. Six small boxes and 3 large boxes contain 75 emu eggs. How many emu eggs are in a large box?

Q84. A tourist shop in Alice Springs sells spoons and caps. If 4 spoons and 7 caps cost $75 and 5 spoons and 9 caps cost $96, how much does a cap cost?

Q85. A bush-walking group has large and small cans for carrying water. The group knows that 3 large and 4 small cans can carry 135 L of water, while 5 large and 2 small cans can carry 155 L of water. What is the carrying capacity of a large and a small can?

Q86. Carpet shampoo is sold in 2 brands, Early Spring and Rose. If 5 containers of Early Spring and 3 containers of Rose cost $17, while 2 containers of Early Spring and 6 containers of Rose cost $14, how much does a container of each brand cost?

Q87. Two families go to the snowfields. The first family hires 3 pairs of skis and 2 pairs of boots for a total cost of $111. The second family hires 4 pairs of skis and 3 pairs of boots for a total cost of $153. How much does it cost to hire a pair of skis.

Q88. The sum of two numbers is 75 and their difference is 13. What are the two numbers?

Q89. In a farmyard there are only chickens and cows. There are 13 animals altogether and between them they have 34 legs. How many cows are there?

Q90. Suppose 3 pencils and 5 erasers cost $1.62;and that 7 pencils and 2 erasers cost $2.04. What is the cost of: (a) a pencil? (b) an eraser?

Q91. From each 2 kg of butter, Shirley can make 4 large and 14 small cakes or she can make 8 of each size. How many grams of butter are needed for: (a) a small cake? (b) a large cake?

Q92. In one year's time John will be twice as old as Peter. Five years ago John was three times as old as Peter. How old are John and Peter now?

Q93. At a tourist shop in Darwin you can buy 8 toy crocodiles and 5 toy camels fora total of $58 and 9 toy crocodiles and 6 toy camels for a total of $67.50. How much does a toy crocodile cost?

SIMULTANEOUS EQUATIONS

Q94. Zac and Zina have $14.70 between them, and Zac's share is three quarters of Zina's. How much money does each have?

Q95. Ten years ago Andrew was four times as old as Linda, and in six year's time he will be twice as old as Linda. What is Andrew's present age?

Q96. Four times the greater of two numbers is 21 more than three times the smaller, and the sum of three times the greater and twice the smaller is 3. Find the numbers.

Q97. Find a fraction which becomes two-thirds when the numerator and denominator are decreased by 1, and becomes four-fifths when the numerator and denominator are increased by 3.

Q98. Margarine is sold in either 250 g or 400 g packets. If a supermarket manager orders 9.8 kg of margarine and receives 29 packets, how many of each type did he receive?

Q99. Split 79 into two parts so that one part may exceed 38 by as much as the other part exceeds 17.

Q100. A motor boat travels 12 km/h upstream against the current and 18 km/h downstream with the current. Find the speed of the current and the speed of the motor boat in still water.

Q101. If Bill gives Peter an hour's start, he overtakes him when they have both walked 12 km. If Peter walks at twice his normal speed he can give Bill an hour's start and overtake him when they have both walked 24 km. Find the speed at which both Bill and Peter walk. (Assume they walk at a constant speed.)

Q102. A test consists of 5 multi-choice items and 8 free response questions. Elise can do it in 34 minutes. If it consisted of 3 multi-choice items and 5 free response questions it would take Elise 21 minutes. All questions in each type were equally difficult. How long does it take for Elise to do each type of question?

Q103. An exercise in a text book is made up of skills questions and problems. Natasha can do 8 skills questions and 3 problems in 28 minutes. She can do 7 skills questions and 5 problems in 34 minutes. If all questions within each type were equally difficult how long does it take Natasha to do one skills question and one problem?

Q104. Terry and Christine carry the shopping in and out of the car every Saturday and all their shopping bags carry the same weight. They can carry all 22 bags in if Terry makes 4 trips and Christine makes 5 trips or if Terry makes 6 trips and Christine makes 2 trips. How many bags does Terry carry in each of his trips.

MATHEMATICAL WORD PROBLEMS

Q105. Baby table and chairs sold at a Discount Store are such that 2 tables and 5 chairs cost $30, while 8 tables and 7 chairs cost $68. How much does 1 table and 1 chair cost?

Q106. Caroline has a train set at home made up of carriages and engines. If she joined together 2 carriages and 5 engines the train set would be 134 cm long. If she joins 4 carriages and 7 engines the train would be 208 cm long. How long is each piece?

Q107. Lance grows lettuces and beetroot in his backyard garden. He grows a total of 43 plants, having 15 more lettuce plants than beetroot plants. How many of each type does he plant?

Q108. Lance decides to plant potatoes and spinach in his garden. In order to reap 4 kg of potatoes and 3 kg of spinach he would need to use up 25m² of land. If he wished to reap 5 kg of potatoes and 7 kgs of spinach, he would need to use up 41m². How much land is need to reap 1 kg of each type of vegetable?

Q109. A 30 litre coffee urn can be filled by pouring in 10 small and 5 large jugs of water. It could also be filled by pouring in 6 small jugs and 7 large jugs of water. What is the size of a small and a large jug of water?

Q110. The daily wages of 5 plumbers and 3 apprentices amount to $1880, and the daily wages of 3 plumbers and 5 apprentices amount to $1640. Find the daily wages of a plumber and an apprentice.

Q111. A note counting machine counts the total number of notes and their total value. On a given day it counted $5 and $10 notes only and 2340 notes had a total value of $12650. How many of each note were counted?

Q112. Two catering firms Latham Foods and Hackett Classics each offer a deal to cater for the Year 10 Formal. Latham Foods offers a fixed charge of $500 plus $7 per person, while Hackett Classics offer a fixed charge of $200 plus $10 per person. The total of their offers came to be exactly equal. How many students were going to the Year 10 Formal?

Q113. Julie has 50 coins in her purse, all of which are 20 cent coins or 10 cent coins. The total value of the coins is $5.50. How many of each type of coin does Julie have in her purse?

Q114. There are 42 questions in a French test. Some are worth 2 marks each and others are worth 3 marks each. How many of each type of questions are there if the total number of marks is 100?

SIMULTANEOUS EQUATIONS

Q115. Margaret and Bill buy 50 roses for their garden. Red roses cost $3 each and yellow roses cost $5 each. If they spend $180 in total how many of each type did they buy?

Q116. The sum of two numbers is 53, and their difference is 19. Find the numbers.

Q117. The difference between two numbers is 34. The sum of the same two numbers is 84. Find the numbers.

Q118. Cassandra thinks of two numbers. If she multiplies the first by 2 and adds the second, she gets 99. The difference between the two numbers is 24. Find the numbers.

Q119. There are 2 roads by which Hannah can get to school. One is 1½ km longer than the other. If Hannah walked to school by the short road at 4 km/h and cycled back home by the long road at 12 km/h, her total travelling time would be 1½ hours. Find the length of the short road.

ANSWERS

1. Golf ball $3 each; Cricket ball $7 each.
2. Sweet corn 3 kgs per hectare; beetroot 5 kgs per hectare
3. Kangaroo 8 units; Emu 3 units
4. Arthritis booklet 16 pages; Hearing loss booklet 12 pages
5. 34;15
6. 59;25
7. 82
8. 12;3
9. 41;13
10. 46 and 11
11. Bream 10 kg; Tuna 15 kg
12. Pig pen 8m; Horse yard 12m
13. 6m
14. $247
15. 12
16. 5.5;
17. 19m; 247 sq m
18. 50¢; 20¢
19. 35; 40
20. 80¢; $1.25
21. $1.20; $2.50
22. Apples $5.00; Oranges $6.00
23. Car $4100; Motor cycle $850
24. 26;16
25. 29;17
26. Horse $460; Cow $320
27. Egg 50¢; banana 30¢
28. 7; 5 7 x $10, 5 x $2
29. 50¢
30. 8
31. 3
32. 10; -2
33. 12 and 30
34. 16 and 6
35. 8 and 3
36. length = 5 cm; width = 2 cm
37. Icy pole : $1.10, drinks : $3
38. Cake : $2.50, coffee : $6
39. Bat : $50; ball : $5
40. Shirt : $7; gloves : $15
41. Father is 39; daughter is 13
42. Adult : $2.50; Child : $1.50

SIMULTANEOUS EQUATIONS

43. 7; 13
44. Apple : 9¢; orange : 6¢
45. Jacket $15, Trousers $6 each to clean
46. Rodney has $9; Jennifer has $3
47. 55
48. 23
49. 4 hours; 250 km
50. 3
51. ¾
52. 18
53. AB = 8m; AC = 10m; BC = 6m
54. 7 x 3-legged; 6 x 4-legged tables
55. 1450 x 20¢; 620 x 50¢
56. Bubble gum : 10¢; chocolate : 20¢
57. Cow : $100; sheep : $30
58. Gloves : $20; Shirts : $12
59. 150 adults; 400 children
60. 42 cows
61. 9; 81
62. 98; 7
63. length = 8 cm; breadth = 4 cm
64. length = 9 cm; breadth = 6 cm
65. 35; 6
66. 35; 8
67. sides = 10; diagonals = 35
68. sides = 6; diagonals = 9
69. Sum = 300; (n = 24)
70. 25; 15
71. 5; 7
72. $\dfrac{5}{6}$
73. Bob = 14 years; Alice = 36 years
74. 30 years; 3 years
75. $\dfrac{9}{11}$
76. 21; 12
77. 11½; 4½
78. 13; 52
79. 23¢; 15¢
80. Orange 50¢; banana 30 ¢
81. $x = 30$; $y = 10$
82. $7
83. 11
84. $9
85. Large : 25L; small : 15L
86. Early Spring : $2.50; Rose : $1.50
87. $27
88. 44; 31
89. 4
90. 24¢; 18¢
91. (a) 100 g; (b) 150 g
92. John is 23; Peter is 11

93. $3.50
94. Zac has $6.30; Zina has $8.40
95. Andrew is 42. Linda is 18
96. 3; -3
97. $\frac{5}{7}$
98. 12 x 250 g packets; 17 x 400 g packets
99. 50; 29
100. Current is 3 km/h; Still water travel is 15 km/h
101. Peter walks at 4 km/h; Bill walks at 6 km/h
102. Multi-choice 2 mins each; free response 3 mins each
103. Skills question 2 mins; problem 4 mins; total 6 mins
104. 3
105. Table $5; chair $4
106. Carriages 17 cm; engines 20 cm
107. 29 lettuce; 14 beetroot
108. Potatoes 4m²; spinach 3 m²
109. Small 1½ L; large 3 L
110. Plumber $280; apprentice $160
111. 2150 $5 notes; and 190 $10 notes
112. 100
113. 5 x 20¢ coins; 45 x 10¢ coins
114. 26 x 2-mark questions; 16 x 3-mark questions
115. 35 x red roses; 15 x yellow roses
116. 17 and 36
117. 25 and 59
118. 41 and 17
119. $4\frac{1}{8}$ km

Ω
QUADRATIC EQUATIONS

Q1. A triangle has an area of 132 cm². If its base is 10 cm more than its height, what is the length of its base?

Q2. If I square the age I was 4 years ago and add my age in 2 years time, the answer is 162.

MATHEMATICAL WORD PROBLEMS

Q3. A rectangle has length 3 cm more than its width. If the area is 40 square cms, find the length.

Q4. An envelope has an area of 84 cm². If the length is 5 cm longer than the width, find the dimensions of the envelope.

Q5. A cardboard square of side 6m has a rectangle cut out of it. The length of this rectangle is 1 m more than its width. The area left over comprises 16 m² of cardboard. What are the length and width of the rectangle that has been removed?

Q6. The sum of a positive number and its square is 90. Find the number.

Q7. The sum of 2 positive numbers is 7 and their product is 12. Find the smaller of the numbers.

Q8. The difference between a positive integer and its square is 56. Find the number.

Q9. The base of a triangle is 5 cm longer than its height. If the area of the triangle is 7 cm², find the length of the base.

Q10. A farmer wishes to build three small stockyards as shown.

He has 200m of fencing. Find the length (L) and the breadth (B) if the area enclosed is greatest.

Q11. A triangle, whose base is 10 cm more than its altitude has an area of 168 cm². What is the length of its base?

Q12. Dominic is 2 years younger than Justin. The square of Dominic's age plus Justin's age is 158. How old are the two boys?

Q13. A rectangle is such that its length is 3 cm more than its breadth. If the area of the rectangle is 18 cm², find the dimensions of the rectangle.

Q14. A triangle is such that its base length and height (in cm) are equal. If the area of the triangle is 8 cm², find the height of the triangle.

Q15. A triangle having equal base length and height (in cm) has an area of 32 cm². Find the length of the base of the triangle.

Q16. The sum of a natural number and its square is 12. Find the number.

Q17. The sum of a natural number and its square is 20. Find the number.

Q18. The product of two consecutive natural numbers is 156. Find the numbers.

QUADRATIC EQUATIONS

Q19. The product of two consecutive natural numbers is 342. Find the numbers.

Q20. The product of two consecutive *even* natural numbers is 168. Find the numbers.

Q21. The product of two consecutive *odd* numbers is 195. Find the numbers.

Q22. If one less than the reciprocal of a certain positive number is 1 more than the number, find the number.

Q23. If the reciprocal of a certain positive number is one less than twice that number, find the number.

Q24. A right-angled triangle is drawn so that one side is 14 cm longer than the other, and the hypotenuse is 26 cm. Find the dimensions of the triangle.

Q25. A right-angled triangle is drawn so that the hypotenuse is 8 cm longer than the shortest side. If the third side is 16 cm, find the dimensions of the triangle.

Q26. An envelope has an area of 221 cm². The length is 4 cm longer than its width. Find the dimensions of the envelope.

Q27. A wooden table has an area of 132 cm². If its length is 1 cm longer than its width, find the dimensions of the table.

Q28. A postage stamp is 3 times longer than it is wide. Its area is 75 cm². What are its dimensions.

Q29. Anita went to the record shop to buy compact discs, normally priced at $18. The shop was running a special so that you only pay $17 if you buy 1, $16 each if you buy 2, $15 each if you buy 3 etc. (i.e. one dollar off for each one Anita buys up to 9 discs). Anita spent $77. How many did she buy?

Q30. The garden centre charges $20 each for camellias but is giving a special by which you only pay $19 for 1, $18 for 2 etc. (i.e. $1 off for every one you buy up to 8 camellias). If Wendy spent $91 at the garden centre, how many camellias did she buy?

Q31. Flash Willie's Menswear is having a sale on trousers, normally priced at $80 each. If you buy one you pay $77, if you buy 2 you pay $74 each, if you buy 3 you pay $71 each (i.e. $3 off for each one you buy up to 20 trousers.). Bruno felt that this was a good deal and spent $517. How many trousers did Bruno buy?

Q32. A land developer subdivides a block of land into a number of small blocks. All blocks are sold at the same price, giving her a total of $450000. Afterwards she calculates that if she had made the blocks slightly larger (reducing the number of blocks by 1) and increased the price per block by $10000, she would have made a total of $480000. Into how many blocks did she divide her land?

Q33. Danny and Diana are two hikers. Danny walks at 3 km/h and Diana walks at 4 km/h. Danny is exactly 5 km due west of Diana. They start walking at precisely the same moment. Danny walks due east and Diana walks due south. What is the shortest distance between the two walkers?

Q34. To make some clothes Rosetta bought a certain amount of fabric for $240. She could have gone to a dearer fabric shop where they charged $4 per metre more, but Rosetta would have got 3 m less fabric for the same amount of money. How many metres did she purchase?

Q35. A painting for sale at an art show is 24 cm by 20 cm. It is surrounded by a frame of uniform width whose area is 416 cm^2. What is the uniform width of the frame?

Q36. A right angled triangle angle has an area of 96 cm^2. One side adjacent to the right angle is 4 cm longer than the other side adjacent to the right angle. Find the lengths of each of the three sides.

Q37. A fraction is such that the numerator is seven less than the square of the denominator. If six is added to the numerator and one to the denominator, the result is 2. Find the fraction.

Q38. A fraction is such that the numerator is one less than the square of the denominator. If two is added to the numerator and eight to the denominator, the result is $\frac{1}{2}$. Find the fraction.

Q39. A father's age is five years more than the square of his son's age. In twenty years' time the father will be twice as old as his son. What are the father's and the son's ages now?

Q40. A mother's age is two years less than three times her daughter's age. If ten years ago the mother's age was the square of the daughter's age, what are their ages now?

Q41. A gardener plants 600 cabbage plants. The number of plants in each row is 10 more than twice the number of rows. If equal numbers of cabbages were planted in each row, how many rows did he plant?

Q42. After a certain number of tests I have scored a total of 180 marks. In the next two tests I did no work and consequently scored zero for each and reduced my average by 3. How many tests did I do altogether?

QUADRATIC EQUATIONS

Q43. A motor boat can travel 36 km up-stream and back again in 5 hours. If the speed of the current is 3 km/h, find the speed of the boat in still water.

Q44. Bob takes 2 hours longer to build a table than Paul takes. If they work together they could build the table in 2 hours 24 minutes. How long would Paul take working alone?

Q45. A rectangular swimming pool is 12 m long by 6 m wide. It is surrounded by pavement of uniform width, the area of the pavement being $\frac{7}{8}$ of the area of the pool. How wide is the pavement?

Q46. The expenses of a bus trip for a group of school children were $144. If an additional 6 children area taken each child will pay $1.20 less. How many children were there in the original group?

Q47. A sail maker bought two lengths of canvas for $720 each from two different distributors. One length was 9 m shorter than the other but cost him $18 more per metre. How many metres of each did he buy?

Q48. Two trains travel at constant speeds over the same 300 km of track. One of the trains travels 10 km/h faster than the other and takes 1 hour less to complete the trip. Find the speed of each train.

Q49. Amy took $5.00 to buy oranges. She discovered that the price had changed and was 4 cents per orange dearer than she had expected. Consequently she bought 5 fewer oranges and received 20 cents change. What price did Amy pay for the oranges?

Q50. A rectangular garden is to have 60 m of concrete edging around its outside, ie around its perimeter. If the area enclosed is to be 200 m², find the dimensions of the garden.

Q51. The number of diagonals (N) that can be drawn in an n-sided polygon is found by the formula N = $\frac{1}{2}$n (n-3). Find the number of sides in a polygon which has 9 diagonals.

Q52. I buy a toy for $k and sell it for $39 making a profit of k% on the cost price. Find the cost price of the toy.

Q53. In a number of innings a cricketer scores 240 runs. At his next time at batting he scores 7 runs and thus reduces his average by 1 run. Find the number of innings he took to score the 240 runs.

Q54. I travel 200 km at a steady speed. Had I travelled 5 km/h faster I would have saved 2 hours on the trip. Find my speed.

MATHEMATICAL WORD PROBLEMS

Q55. The square of a number and four times the number is 60. What is the number?

Q56. A carpet is placed in a room 6 m by 4 m, leaving a boarder of uniform width all the way round it. If the area of the carpet is 8 m², find this uniform width.

Q57. What positive number is exceeded by its square by 42?

Q58. The difference of two positive numbers is 3 and the sum of their squares is 117. What are the numbers?

Q59. The length of a room exceeds its breadth by 3 m and its area is 180 m². What are its dimensions?

Q60. The sum of two numbers is 9 and the sum of their squares is 41. Find the numbers.

Q61. A lawn is 30 m long and 20 m wide and is surrounded by a path of uniform width whose area is 600 m². Find the width of the path.

Q62. The product of two consecutive even numbers is 80. What are the numbers?

Q63. The sum of a number and its square is twice the next highest number; find the number.

Q64. The product of two numbers which differ by 4 is 45. Find the numbers.

Q65. The width of a room is 4 m less than its length and its area is 192 m². What are the dimensions of the room?

Q66. A number is multiplied by the number which exceeds it by 6 and the product is 55. Find the number.

Q67. The units' digit of a number is 5 less then the square of the tens' digit. Find the number if the sum of the digits is 7.

Q68. What positive number when increased by 45 is 27 less than its square?

Q69. A motorist travels 810 km in (y+3) hours at an average speed of y km an hour. Find her average speed.

Q70. Two positive numbers differ by 4 and the sum of their squares is 106. Find the two numbers.

Q71. A certain fraction is added to its reciprocal and the result is $2\frac{9}{28}$. What is the fraction?

Q72. A carpet 12 m long and 9 m wide is placed in the centre of a room and a boarder of uniform width has to be stained around the carpet. If the area stained is 162 m², what is the width of the boarder?

QUADRATIC EQUATIONS

Q73. The square of a positive number when multiplied by 3 is four times the number which follows it. What is the number?

Q74. The base of a triangle, of area 24 m², is 2 m less than the altitude of the triangle. Find the altitude of the triangle.

Q75. Of three consecutive odd positive numbers the product of the first and the third is 7 more than 10 times the second of them. Find the numbers.

Q76. A train travels 300 km at a uniform rate; if the speed had been 5 km an hour more, the journey would have taken two hours less; find the speed at which the train travels.

Q77. The sum of the reciprocals of two consecutive numbers is $\frac{11}{30}$. Find the numbers.

Q78. Gerard cycles 108 km at a uniform speed and finds that he could have made the journey in $4\frac{1}{2}$ hours less had he travelled 2 km an hour faster: at what speed did he travel?

Q79. Ken bought articles for $72 and found that if he had bought 6 more for the same amount he would have paid $1 less for each. How many articles did he buy?

Q80. A train travels a distance of 60 km at a uniform speed. If it had travelled 10 km an hour faster it would have taken half an hour less for the journey. Find the speed of the train.

Q81. Two trucks each travel a distance of 330 km, one at x km per hour, the other at ($x + 5$) km per hour. The faster takes half an hour less than the other for the whole distance. What are their speeds?

Q82. I plan to travel for 60 km at a certain speed. I find that if I were to travel 4 km/h faster I would save 4 hours on the trip. At what speed did I originally plan to travel?

Q83. One number exceeds another by 2. The sum of their squares is 34. Find the numbers, assuming both are positive.

Q84. Some business people went to breakfast and the total was $38. One of the business people was a guest and did not have to pay, meaning each of the others had to pay 10 cents more than the cost of their meal. How many business people went to breakfast?

Q85. A tradesman takes a certain amount of time to make 24 toys, while an apprentice takes 4 hours longer to make 24 toys. Together they make 5 toys in an hour. How long does each take to make the 24 toys.

MATHEMATICAL WORD PROBLEMS

Q86. John walked 35 km at a certain speed. Had he increased his speed by 2 km/h he would have saved 2 hours. At what speed did he travel?

Q87. Helen bought a certain number of glasses for a total amount of $45. She then sold some, each for $1 more than she paid for them. She received a total of $52 from selling these glasses and still had 2 glasses left for herself. How many glasses did she buy originally?

Q88. A mushroom farmer has an order to send 70 kg of mushrooms to the markets in standard cases. If he uses larger cases that each hold 2 kg more he would use 4 less cases. What is the capacity of the standard cases?

Q89. The exporting of 288 kg of frozen lobsters is done in crates. A new type of crate that holds an extra 4 kg would enable the exporter to use 6 less crates. What is the capacity of these new crates?

Q90. A freeway has to have 6300 m of sound proof fencing erected along its side, using certain panels. If a new different panel which is 1 m wider was used, 1050 less panels would have to be used altogether. What is the width of the original panels and the new panels?

Q91. A farmer has to connect a number of irrigation pipes to link his property to a creek, a distance of 315 m. If he could use a new different type of pipe, 2 m longer, he would have to use 18 less pipes. What is the length of the original pipe?

Q92. A council placed railway sleepers around a park, a total distance of 270 m. Had they used a longer railway sleeper, 2 m longer than the original, they would have had to use 36 less railway sleepers altogether. How many railway sleepers did the council use? How many would they have used if they had used the larger sleepers?

Q93. A perfume company has to place 105 ml of perfume into little bottles for sale. They could have placed the perfume into bottles each of which hold 20 ml more than the little bottles, and thus used 4 less bottles in total. What is the capacity of the little bottles?

Q94. An industrial process requires 4400 litres of water being poured into a vat from buckets. A new process that uses buckets which have a capacity of 3L greater than the original one, would require using 330 less buckets in total. Find the capacity of the buckets in the new process.

QUADRATIC EQUATIONS

Q95. A strawberry farmer wants to plant 576 m² of strawberries in a number of beds. If he increases the area of each bed by 1 m² he would need 8 less beds. What would be the area of each of these new, larger beds?

Q96. A fence is 12 m long and is built using sheets of galvanised iron of equal width. If the sheets had been 0.2 m wider, 2 less sheets would have been required. What is the width of the sheets used on the fence?

Q97. After a certain number of tests Ivan scored a total of 160 marks. However he did no work after that and scored zero for each of the next two tests. This reduced his average by 4. How many tests did Ivan sit altogether?

Q98. A chemical company sells 105 L in standard drums. If they sold the chemical in large drums each of which hold 20 litres more than the standard drums they could have used 4 less drums in total. What is the capacity of the standard drums?

Q99. Two positive numbers differ by 4 and the sum of their squares is 136. Find the numbers.

Q100. A carpet 12 m long and 9 m wide is placed in the centre of an auditorium. A border of uniform width has to be stained around the carpet. If the area stained is 232 m², find the width of the border.

Q101. What must be the dimensions of a rectangle to have an area of 125 m² and a perimeter of 60 m?

ANSWERS

1. 22 cm
2. 16 years
3. 8 cm
4. length = 12 cm
   width = 7 cm
5. length = 5 m
   width = 4 m
6. 9
7. 3
8. 8
9. 7 cm
10. L = 50, B = 25
11. 24 cm
12. Dominic 12,
    Justin 14
13. L = 6, B = 3
14. 4 cm
15. 8 cm
16. 3
17. 4
18. 12, 13
19. 18, 19
20. 12, 14
21. 13, 15
22. $\sqrt{2}-1$
23. 1
24. 10, 24, 26
25. 12, 16, 20
26. 13 cm x 17 cm
27. 12 cm x 11 cm
28. 15 cm x 5 cm
29. 7
30. 7
31. 11
32. 9
33. 4 km
34. 15
35. 4 cm
36. 12 cm, 16 cm, 20 cm
37. $\dfrac{2}{3}$
38. $\dfrac{3}{2}$
39. 30, 5
40. 16, 46

QUADRATIC EQUATIONS

41. 15 rows
42. 12 tests
43. 15 km/h
44. 4 hours
45. $\dfrac{3}{2}$ m
46. 24
47. 24 m, 15 m
48. 50 km/h, 60 km/h
49. 24 cents
50. 20 m x 10 m
51. 6 sides
52. $30
53. 12 innings
54. 20 km/h
55. 6 or 10
56. 1m
57. 7
58. 6, 9
59. Length = 15 m, Breadth = 12 m
60. 5, 4
61. 5 m
62. 8, 10
63. 2
64. 5, 9
65. Length = 16 m, Width = 12 m
66. 5
67. 34
68. 9
69. 27 km/h
70. 9 and 5
71. $\dfrac{4}{7}$ or $\dfrac{7}{4}$
72. 3 m
73. 2
74. 8 m
75. 9, 11, 13
76. 25 km/h
77. 5, 6
78. 6 km/h
79. 18
80. 30 km/h
81. 55 km/h, 60 km/h
82. 6 km/h
83. 3, 5
84. 20
85. 8 hours and 12 hours
86. 5 km/h
87. 15
88. 5 kg
89. 16 kg
90. 2 m and 3 m

MATHEMATICAL WORD PROBLEMS

91. 5 m
92. 90, 54
93. 15 ml
94. 8 L
95. 9 m²
96. 1 m

97. 10 tests
98. 15 L
99. 6 and 10
100. 4 m
101. 5 m by 25 m

Ω
RATIO, RATES, MIXTURES AND MOVING

Q1. You scored 135 marks out of a possible 150. Express this as a percentage.

Q2. If Alex scored 85% in his Maths test, how many marks did he score out of a possible 160?

Q3. Out of every 40 vehicles which cross a bridge, 25 are cars, 9 are trucks and the rest are buses. What percentage of vehicles are the buses?

Q4. An estate agent receives 6% commission on the sale of every house. What does she receive on a house sold for $131 250?

Q5. A merchant sells goods which cost $240 for $290. What percentage is her profit of the cost price? What percentage is the profit of her selling price ? (to the nearest whole per cent)

Q6. The stamp duty which has to be paid by someone buying property is 1½% of the purchase price. What would be the amount of stamp duty paid by the buyer on a house worth $250 000?

Q7. I am allowed 15% discount on all items in a department store. How much do I pay altogether if I buy a television set marked at $357, a CD player marked at $224 and an electric shaver marked at $32?

Q8. If the premiums for insuring goods for transport by rail are at the rate of 3¾%, how much would it cost to insure a consignment of goods whose value is declared to be $1700?

Q9. By selling goods at $2.60 a storekeeper makes 30% profit. At what price should she sell them to make a profit of 40%?

Q10. In a school 16% of the pupils are more than 15 years old and 12% are less than 13 years old. There are 288 pupils in the age-group 13-15. How many pupils are there in the school?

Q11. Suppose 5% of a tomato crop is damaged by frost and later 20% of the remainder is damaged by rain. Altogether 38 cases were able to be packed. How many would have been packed if there had been no damage?

Q12. A picture frame is aesthetically pleasing if the ratio of the width to length is 5:8. What should be the width of a picture frame whose length is 56 cm?

Q13. Emily and Jake invest in a company in the ratio 4:3. If Emily's profit from the company is $28 360, how much will Jake receive?

Q14. In creating a wood filler substitute, clean sawdust and white glue is mixed in the ratio 5:2 by volume. How much glue must be added to 22 ml of sawdust to form this substitute?

Q15. The ratio of the circumference of a circle to its diameter is about 3.14 : 1. What is the circumference of a bicycle wheel which has a 65 cm diameter? (answer to the nearest cm)

RATIO, RATES, MIXTURES AND MOVING

Q16. One season the Canberra Cannons outscored their opponents by a ratio of 8:5. If the Cannons scored 328 goals, how many goals did the opponents score?

Q17. Two numbers, in the ratio 2:3, have the sum of 140. What are the numbers?

Q18. In a basketball game, Dylan, Joshua and Andrew scored a total of 72 points. The ratio of Dylan's points to Joshua's points was 2:7 and Joshua's points to Andrew's points was 7:3. How many points did each score?

Q19. Grace, Skye and Rose share the rent on their townhouse. Due to differences in room sizes, the ratio of Grace's rent to Skye's rent is 4:3 and Grace's rent to Rose's rent is 2:1. Find each girl's rent if the fortnightly rent is $540.

Q20. Laughing gas consists of nitrogen and oxygen in the ratio 28:16 by mass. How much oxygen is contained in 22g of laughing gas?

Q21. Heavy water consists of hydrogen (an isotope of hydrogen) and oxygen which have combined in the ratio 1:4 by mass. What mass of oxygen is contained in 60g of heavy water?

Q22. Silicon and oxygen combine in the ratio 7:8 by mass to produce ordinary sand. What mass of silicon is contained in 45g of sand?

Q23. Salt consists of sodium and chlorine in the ratio 23 : 35.5 by mass. What mass of chlorine is contained in 117g of salt?

Q24. Ammonia consists of nitrogen and hydrogen combined in the ratio 14:3 by mass. How many grams of ammonia contain 56g of nitrogen?

Q25. Moth balls consist of carbon and hydrogen which have combined in the ratio 15:1 by mass. If the carbon from 48g of moth balls could be obtained, what would be its mass?

Q26. (a) Sand is composed of silicon and oxygen in the ratio 7:8 by mass. What mass of oxygen is contained in 90g of sand?

(b) Dry ice consists of carbon and oxygen in the ratio 3:8 by mass. Using oxygen obtained in part (a) above, what mass of dry ice would be created if sufficient carbon were available?

Q27. A Swimming pool 50m long has a bottom which slopes uniformly from a depth of 1.5m at one end to a depth of 3m at the deep end. Find the depth at the 10m, 15m and 25m marks measured from the shallow end.

MATHEMATICAL WORD PROBLEMS

Q28. Last season, a cereal farmer grew wheat, barley and oats. If he harvested x tonnes of wheat, y tonnes of barley and 150 tonnes of oats, find x and y, given the ratio of wheat : barley was 3:2 and the tonnage of barley harvested was 60% more than that of oats harvested.

Q29. The heights of three children are in the ratio of 9:8:7. If the tallest child is 40 cm taller than the shortest, find the height of each child.

Q30. The weights of 3 men are in the ratio heavy : medium : light = 4:3:x. The heaviest man weighs twice as much as the lightest and the sum of the weights of all three men is 270 kg. Find the weight of each man.

Q31. Milk is sold in large, medium and small cartons of capacities 1 litre, 600 ml and 250 ml respectively.

(a) Find the ratio of the capacities of the containers.

(b) If a delicatessen owner orders 63 litres of milk and insists that the ratio of cartons is large : medium : small is 4:3:2, how many of each type of carton will he receive?

Q32. Cement costs $85 a tonne, gravel $25 a tonne and sand $30 a tonne. Superior concrete consists of gravel, sand and cement in the ratio 4:2:1 by weight and one cubic metre of this mixture weighs approximately 1.2 tonne. What will the concrete in a factory floor cost if the floor is 20m long, and 45m wide and 15 cm thick?

Q33. Wayne catches two buses to work. The first leg of the trip consists of 12 minutes at 35 kph; and the second leg consists of 20 kilometres at 50 kph. Ignoring changeover times, what is the average speed for the entire trip?

Q34. The ratio of the mean population density of Asia to that of Australia is 30:1. If the mean in Asia is 90 people per km^2, what is the mean in Australia?

Q35. At a local church there were 120 baptisms in a year. The ratio of males to females was 7:5. How many girls were baptized?

Q36. An athlete can run the 100m sprint in 19 seconds. What is this speed in kilometres per hour? (answer to 2 decimal places)

Q37. If $1 (Australian currency) is worth 70c (U.S. currency) and you had $105 (U.S). How many Australian dollars should you receive if you converted your $105 (U.S.) into Australian currency?

RATIO, RATES, MIXTURES AND MOVING

Q38. Mr Sheedy walks from Coburg to Victoria markets at a speed of 6 km/h. He leaves Coburg at the same time as the tram, which has a speed of 18 km/h. When the tram reaches Victoria markets it immediately turns back and heads for Coburg, meeting Mr Sheedy 4.5 km from Victoria markets. What is the distance from Coburg to Victoria markets?

Q39. For every 2 jobs lost in a local cannery, there will be 5 other jobs lost in the surrounding region. If there are 124 workers in the cannery, how many other jobs would be lost in the surrounding region if the cannery closed down?

Q40. Martin rows downstream at 5 km/h and back up stream at 3 km/h. If he rowed x kilometres downstream, how long did the total trip take? If the trip took 72 minutes, how far downstream did he go?

Q41. The lengths of the sides of a triangle are in the ratios 3:4:5. If the perimeter of the triangle is 6m, what is the length of the longest side?

Q42. Mr Miller left an estate of $18 720 to 3 charities to be divided among them in the ratios 2:3:4. How much money was received by each charity?

Q43. How could $1 050 be divided between 2 people in the ratio 4:3. How could it be divided between 3 people in the ratios 3:5:6?

Q44. Two numbers are in the ratio 3:4. If 4 were added to each number the ratio of the resulting numbers would be 5:6. What are the numbers?

Q45. Two men travel by car, one averaging 45 km/h and the other 35 km/h. The faster, travelled 30 kilometres further than the slower, and made the trip in 2 hours less time. How far did each man travel?

Q46. When emptying a 1 kg bag of sugar, 20g of sugar are wasted. How much sugar must be purchased to get 49 kg of useable sugar?

Q47. Sarah's coin collection totals $18.45. She has 35 times as many 1 cent pieces as she has 10 cent pieces. How many coins are there altogether?

Q48. The cash box at the shop has 100 more 10 cent coins than 50 cent coins. If the value of the two types of coins in the cash box, is exactly $22.00, how many 50 cent coins are there?

Q49. David's rectangular backyard is 8m longer than it is wide. The perimeter is 44m. Sue's backyard is 6m longer but 2m narrower than David's. Find the dimensions of their backyards.

MATHEMATICAL WORD PROBLEMS

Q50. A tap drips water at the rate of 15 ml/h. How much water is wasted in one week?

Q51. Have you ever paid a bill using only 5 cent coins? Vanessa did, but she found that if she used only 10 cent coins she would have used 25 fewer coins. How much was the bill?

Q52. Find the speed of each animal in both metres per second and km per hour.

(a) a dingo ran 300 metres in 40 seconds

(b) a deer travelled a distance of 300 metres in 24 seconds.

Q53. During the recent football season the Raiders lost twice as many games as they won, but they did tie 6 more games than they lost. If during the season they played a total of 26 games, then how many games did they tie?

Q54. Every tonne of brown coal contains 25 kg of stone. How much coal must be purchased to obtain 78 tonnes of good coal?

Q55. 100 litres of a solution contains 15% salt by volume. How much of the 100 litres should be withdrawn and replaced by pure water to make the solution 10% salt?

Q56. Mimi has 35 stamps. Some are valued at 2¢ each, others at 5¢ and the remainder at 10¢. She has 3 times as many 5¢ stamps as she has 2¢ stamps and the total value of all 3 types is $1.89. How many of each stamp has she?

Q57. A coffee blender mixes brand A costing $3 per kg with brand B costing $4 per kg. How many kg of each brand does he have to blend to make 50 kg of coffee valued at $3.60 per kg?

Q58. I have 13 kg of almonds which sell at $5 per kg. How many kg of cashews which sell at $12 per kg should be added to get a mixture of the two nuts which would sell at $7.45 per kg?

Q59. Gas Works shares pay a dividend of 9% and Electricity Trust shares pay a dividend of 11%. John invests $1 500 more on Electricity Trust shares than on Gas Works shares and his total receipts from the two investments is $1 475. How much did he invest in Gas Works shares?

Q60. Mrs Nugent invests $4000 at 10% and $6000 at 12%. How much should she invest at 15% so that her annual income is 13% of the entire investment?

Q61. Joel can mow a lawn in 15 minutes. Sarah has a smaller mower, but when she helps Joel to mow the lawn it takes them 10 minutes. How long would Sarah take to mow the lawn by herself?

RATIO, RATES, MIXTURES AND MOVING

Q62. How much water must be added to 5 litres of an 8% salt solution to make a 5% salt solution?

Q63. Approximately half of the 120,000 Australians that die each year, die from either cancer or heart disease. The ratio of cancer-related deaths to heart-disease-related deaths is about 2 : 3. Based on these figures, approximately how many cancer-related deaths will there be this year?

Q64. Tickets at a hockey match cost $3, $5 and $7.50. The number of $5 tickets sold was 3 times more than the number of $3 tickets sold and 500 less than the number of $7.50 tickets sold. If the total gate receipts were $42 225, how many of each type of ticket was sold?

Q65. Alice deposited an amount of money in the bank at 10% for a year. If she had invested $240 more at 9%, the interest earned in a year would have been the same. How much money did she invest in the bank?

Q66. To dye the drapes Tony made 10kg of dye which had only a concentration of 8% colouring. He learned that the proper concentration had to be 25%. How much water needs to be evaporated so that the final concentration will be 25%?

Q67. My backyard is enclosed by a fence that has a perimeter of 168m. The fence is 3m high. If the length is 36m more than twice the width, how wide is my backyard?

Q68. For a concert the school sold 834 tickets. Almost 353 tickets were sold the first night. If the number of student tickets was 48 more than twice the number of adult tickets sold, how many students attended the concert?

Q69. The ratio of hot dogs to pies sold at a football match is 3 : 5. If a total of 750 pies were sold, how many hot dogs were sold?

Q70. If a car uses 12 litres of petrol to travel 96 km, how many litres of petrol will it use to travel 12 km?

Q71. If an order of 7 packs of French fries cost $3.85, find the cost of an order of 4 packs of French fries.

Q72. Peter noticed that when he had 15 Zebra finches in his aviary they emptied the seed container in 6 days. How long would the same quantity of seed last if 3 more Zebra finches were added to the aviary?

Q73. It took a team of twelve cleaners 4 hours 30 minutes to clean an office block of 20 rooms.

(a) How many cleaners would be needed if 5 more rooms were opened up in the block and the total cleaning time was to remain unchanged?

(b) If the cleaning time for the 20 rooms had to be reduced to 3 hours, how many more cleaners would need to be employed?

Q74. Rachel is 160 cm tall. At a certain time of the day she notes that the length of her shadow is 100 cm whilst the shadow of the gum tree in the backyard is 15.8m long. How tall is the gum tree?

Q75. A window cleaning contractor can clean all the windows in a building in 5 days using a team of 8 people. This year the client wants the job completed in 4 days. How many cleaners are required?

Q76. Two tractors with plough units can finish ploughing a paddock in 9 hours.

(a) How long would it take 3 tractors with plough units to do the same job?

(b) If the third unit did not begin working until the first two were half finished, how long would it take them to finish?

Q77. A motorist named Matthew sets out each day at 8.10 am to drive to work in the next town which he reaches at 8.55 am at his normal speed of 80 km/h. One day he leaves 5 minutes late. At what speed must he travel to arrive on time?

Q78. A large store has its lights on for 18 hours each day and during a one year period it is necessary to replace 1 500 globes. If the lights were turned on for 3 hours less each day, estimate the number of globes which would require replacing over the same period.

Q79. Each day, on his way to school, Jamie is passed by a train going in the opposite direction, He notes that when the train has 6 carriages (including the engine) it takes 9 seconds to pass him. One day it took 15 seconds to pass. If Jamie and the train always move at the same speed, calculate the number of carriages on the train that day.

Q80. Speedie can run twice as fast as Slowie. They start at the same point and run in opposite directions for 40 minutes and the distance between them is then 16 km. How fast does Speedie run?

Q81. A freight train leaves a city at 6 pm travelling at 50 km/h and at 9 pm a passenger train leaves the same city on an adjacent track at 100 km/h. How long will it take for the passenger train to overtake the freight train?

RATIO, RATES, MIXTURES AND MOVING

Q82. A car leaves a country town travelling at 60 km/h. Two hours later a second car leaves the same country town and catches up with the first car in 5 hours. Find the speed of the second car.

Q83. A girl rides her bicycle to see her grandma at an average rate of 10 km/h. Waiting at grandma's is a taxi which returns her home immediately. If the speed of the taxi is 80 km/h and the total travelling time for the entire trip is 45 minutes, how far is it to grandma's?

Q84. A motor cyclist makes a trip of 500 km. If he increased his speed by 10 km/h he could have covered 600 km in the same time. Determine his original speed.

Q85. Two runners leave cities which are 30 km apart. One runner runs at a speed which is 3 km/h faster than the other. If they meet after 2 hours, find the speed of each runner.

Q86. Normally I drive to work at 60 km/h. However when I drive at 72 km/h I cut 8 minutes off my time for the trip. What distance do I travel?

Q87. One calm day it took me 4 hours to travel from Camden to Berrima by bicycle. The next day I battled against a head wind of 6 km/h all the way and consequently it took me 2 hours longer to travel the same route. What was my average speed on the calm day?

Q88. As you climb up a mountain in South America, the temperature decreases by 1° for every 100 metres you ascend. If the temperature at the summit is 15°C, what is the temperature 600m lower down the mountain?

Q89. A bus travelling at 65 km/h takes 75 minutes less than a truck travelling at 52 km/h from Albury to Mildura. What is the distance between the two cities?

Q90. Two cyclists leave Goulburn at the same time and travel along the highway. One cyclist travels 2 km/h slower than 3 times the other cyclist's speed. After 4 hours they are 56 km apart. How fast is each cyclist travelling?

Q91. Branko drove from his house in Gympie to his holiday house at 75 km/h and returned at 60 km/h. If the total trip took 12 hours, how far is it from his holiday house to home?

Q92. For a football match two buses leave 20 minutes apart and travel along the same road. If the first bus travels at 66 km/h and the later bus at 77 km/h, how long does it take for the later bus to catch up?

Q93. Mario's speed on his bicycle is 6 km/h faster than he walks. To go to the bowling alley by bicycle he takes 12 minutes, but it takes 30 minutes if he walks. How far is it to the bowling alley?

MATHEMATICAL WORD PROBLEMS

Q94. Beselka's family left the picnic 30 minutes after Hanh's family. Beselka's car went 15 km/h faster than Hanh's car and overtook her in 45 minutes. How fast was Hanh's car travelling?

Q95. For the first part of a bicycle trip of 110 km, a wind of 3 km/h helped the cyclists. If the wind blew for only 4 hours and the trip lasted 6 hours, find the speed of the bicycles.

96. Two planes leave an airport at the same time and fly in opposite direction. Their speeds differ by 150 km/h. After 4 hours, the planes are 3000 km apart. How fast is each plane going?

Q97. Con can row his boat in still water at the speed of 8 km/h. How long would it take him to row his boat 10 km upstream from his dock and back to the dock, if the water in the river flows at a speed of 3 km/h? (answer to the nearest minute).

Q98. Dick flew from Albury to Parkes, a distance of 300 km in 48 minutes and from Parkes to Newcastle, a distance of 450 km, in 1 hour and 15 minutes. Find his average speed for each leg of the trip, giving answers in km/h. Which part of the flight had the faster average speed?

Q99. When the netball club decided the winner of the trophy for the highest number of goals thrown per match the two contenders were:

Denise, who threw 446 goals in 18 matches and

Raelene, who threw 394 goals in 15 matches.

Who won the trophy?

Q100. If Tony averaged 5.6 goals per game in football in 220 games whilst Jason averaged 3.8 goals in 305 games, who kicked the most goals?

Q101. Wayne's average driving speed in the country was 1.6 times his city average. If he had a journey involving 20 km of city driving and 220 km of country driving and the city leg took him 25 minutes, find his total time for the journey.

Q102. At Belconnen recycling plant the ratio of paper : glass : plastic = 13 : 8 : 5 (by weight). If 640 kg. of glass was collected one day, what would you expect the amount of paper to be?

Q103. On a certain day $1.00 (Australian) was worth 72 cents (U.S.) and $1.10 (N.Z.). How many U.S. dollars could be obtained with $1 000 N.Z.?

RATIO, RATES, MIXTURES AND MOVING

Q104. 1 millilitre of water weighs 1 gram.

(a) What is the weight of   (i) 1 litre of water,

(ii) 1 cubic metre of water?

(b) Find the weight of water in tonnes in a rectangular tank 5m by 4m by 3.5m.

Q105. In a 'limited overs' cricket match the fielding side scored 213 runs in 50 overs, and the batting side has scored 154 runs in 35 overs. If they continue to score at the same rate for the remaining 15 overs, would they win?

Q106. An aircraft can fly as far in 4 hours with a 65 km/h wind behind it (following) as it could in 5 hours against the same wind. What is the speed of the aircraft?

Q107. Each side of a square is reduced by ¼ of its length, and the area of the remaining square is 729 cm². What was the area of the original square?

Q108. If I walk to the station at 5 km/h, I shall miss my train by 3 minutes. If I run at 12 km/h, I shall have 4 minutes to spare before the train arrives. How far away is the train station?

Q109. The new railway carriage will each be 30 m long and 3 m wide. A model, on display in Junee, is 12 cm long.

(a) What is the width of the model?

(b) If the model is 1.8 cm high, what is the height of the carriage?

Q110. A wheel of radius 9 cm makes 1000 revolutions in travelling a certain distance. How many revolutions would a wheel of radius 15 cm make in travelling the same distance?

Q111. A mountain climber ascends a mountain at the rate of 600 m per day and descends at 2400 m per day. If the total time for the descent and ascent is 12 days, how high is the mountain?

Q112. Craig washed 15 windows in 2 hours. How many more windows would he have washed had he worked one-third faster and a half-an-hour longer?

Q113. A car has travelled at an average speed of 80 km/h. What speed must it average for the remaining 90 km of the journey if it is to average 75 km/h for its overall journey of 150 km?

MATHEMATICAL WORD PROBLEMS

Q114. There are three pipes leading to a storage tank. Operating separately, one fills the tank in 5 hours, the second one fills the tank in 3 hours and the third one empties the tank in 4 hours. the tank is empty. If the three pipes operate together, how many hours will elapse before the tank starts to overflow?

Q115. Kristy worked 6 hours a day for 5 days and 4 hours on a Saturday. Hours worked on Saturday are regarded as overtime and she is paid 'time-and-a-half'. What are her wages for the week if she is paid at $8.55 per hour?

Q116. A real estate agent charges commission as follows for selling a house:

$2 900 on the first $90 000

3% on the remaining amount.

The real estate agent sold Fran's house for $128 500.

(a) Calculate the commission paid to the real estate agent.

(b) What amount did Fran receive after deducting the real estate agent's fee plus 1% stamp duty on the selling price of the house?

Q117. It is found that a truck uses fuel at 22 litres per 100 km. If the truck travels a distance of 380 km, how much fuel does it use?

Q118. A farmer purchases 60 tonnes of superphosphate to spread over her 400 hectare property. Calculate the rate of application in kg per hectare.

Q119. A sample bag at the show consists of banana candies and jelly beans. Each type of lolly sells for 2 cents each. If the ratio of banana candies to jelly beans in the sample bag is 11:4 and Megan paid $1.80 for her sample bag, how many jelly beans are in Megan's bag?

Q120. A medical centre saw a number of patients today. The ratio of men to women was 3:2 and the ratio of girls to boys is 1:3. There are 24 men and 15 boys. Find the ratio of adults to children.

Q121. A painter charges $150 per day to paint a house. If the job cost $1 350, how many days will it take?

Q122. A farm spray is to be mixed in the ratio of 2 parts chemical to 13 parts water. If a correctly mixed spray contains 143 litres of water, how many litres of chemical was used?

RATIO, RATES, MIXTURES AND MOVING

Q123. The illumination (L) of a light source varies inversely as the square of the distance (D) from the source. At what distance from the source will the illumination be 4 times that of the illumination at a distance of 2 metres from the source?

Q124. To make a brine solution, Louise used a 500 kg container. The brine solution has a concentration of 24%. How much water would she need to add to 50 kg of the brine to decrease the concentration to 10%?

Q125. How many litres of 15% sugar solution must be added to 5 litres of 10% sugar solution to make a 12% sugar solution?

Q126. A rectangular swimming pool is 25 m by 15 m and is filled from pipes which deliver 500 litres of water per minute. How long will it take to rise 10 cm?

Q127. At a children's party, there was a 20L container full of lemon cordial, which contained 15% lemon concentrate. The parents wanted to reduce the strength of the cordial to 9% lemon concentrate by removing some of the original cordial and replacing it with the same amount of pure water. How many litres of the original cordial should the parents have removed in order to bring the concentrate down to 9%?

ANSWERS

1. 90%
2. 136
3. 15%
4. $7 875
5. 21%, 17%
6. $3 750
7. $521.05
8. $63.75
9. $2.80
10. 400
11. 50
12. 35 cm
13. $21 270
14. 8.8 ml
15. 204 cm
16. 205 goals
17. 56, 84
18. Dylan 12, Joshua 42, Andrew 18
19. Grace $240, Skye $180, Rose $120
20. 8g
21. 48g
22. 21g
23. 71g
24. 68g
25. 45g
26. (a) 48g (b) 66g
27. 1.8m, 1.95m, 2.25m
28. $x = 360$, $y = 240$
29. 180 cm, 160 cm, 140 cm
30. 120 kg, 90 kg, 60 kg
31. (a) 20:12:5
    (b) 40 large, 30 medium, 20 small
32. $5 670
33. 45 kph
34. 3 people/km^2
35. 50
36. 18.95 km/h
37. $150 (Australian)

RATIO, RATES, MIXTURES AND MOVING

38. 9 km
39. 310
40. $\frac{8x}{15}$ hours, 2¼ km
41. 2.5 m
42. $4 160, $6 240, $8 320
43. $600, $450, $225, $375, $450
44. 6, 8
45. 450 km, 420 km
46. 50 kg
47. 1476
48. 20
49. David 15m x 7m, Sue 21m x 5m
50. 2520 ml
51. $2.50
52. (a) 7.5 m/sec, 27 km/h
    (b) 12.5 m/sec, 45 km/h
53. 14
54. 80 tonnes
55. 33 ⅓ L
56. 7 x 2¢ stamps, 21 x 5¢ stamps, 7 x 10¢ stamps
57. A 20 kg, B 30 kg
58. 7 kg
59. $6 550
60. $9 000 at 15%
61. 30 minutes
62. 3 litres
63. 24,000
64. 950 x $3 tickets, 2 850 x $5 tickets, 3 350 x $7.50 tickets
65. $2 160
66. 6.8 litres
67. 16 m
68. 572
69. 450
70. 1.5 litres
71. $2.20
72. 5 days
73. (a) 15
    (b) 6
74. 25.28 m
75. 10 cleaners
76. (a) 6 hours
    (b) 7 ½ hours
77. 90 km/h
78. 1 250 globes
79. 10
80. 16 km/h

MATHEMATICAL WORD PROBLEMS

81. 3 hours
82. 84 km/h
83. $6\frac{2}{3}$ km/h
84. 50 km/h
85. 6 km/h, 9 km/h
86. 48 km
87. 18 km/h
88. 21°C
89. 325 km
90. 8 km/h; 22 km/h
91. 400 km
92. 2 hours
93. 2 km
94. 22.5 km/h
95. $16\frac{1}{3}$ km/h
96. 300 km/h, 450 km/h
97. 2 hrs 55 mins
98. Albury to Parkes 375 km/h
    Parkes to Newcastle 360 km/h
    Albury to Parkes
99. Raelene
100. Tony
101. 196.9 min
102. 1040 kgs.
103. $654.55 (US)
104. (a) (i) 1 kg, (ii) 1 tonne
     (b) 70 tonnes
105. Yes
106. 585 km/h
107. 1296 cm²
108. 1 km
109. 1.2 cm, 4.5 cm
110. 600
111. 5760 m
112. 10
113. 72 km/h
114. $3\frac{9}{17}$ hours
115. $307.80
116. (a) $4 055
     (b) $123 160
117. 83.6 litres
118. 150 kg/hectare
119. 24
120. 2:1
121. 9 days
122. 22 litres
123. 1m
124. 70 litres
125. $3\frac{1}{3}$ litres
126. 75 mins
127. 8 litres

Ω
DIOPHANTINE EQUATIONS

Q1. A small factory makes 2 types of jigsaw puzzles, the Dolphin which has 23 pieces and the Galah which has 13 pieces. One day it used 370 pieces in total without any wastage. How many Dolphin Jigsaw puzzles did it make?

Q2. Trudi bought 50 items at the local post office for a total price of $28.00. Each card cost 40 cents, each stamp 45 cents and each notebook cost 95 cents. She bought more than 10 of each item and bought fewer notebooks than stamps. How many of each item did she buy?

Q3. A Cabinet maker has 45 table legs all of which he uses to make 3-legged and 4-legged tables. He makes more 4-legged tables than 3-legged tables. How many of each does he make?

MATHEMATICAL WORD PROBLEMS

Q4. An electronics company has a contract with a school to repair Data Projectors for $17 each and Camcorders for $25 each. If, for one day's work it charged the school $160, how many of each type of appliance did the company repair?

Q5. A tour company uses coaches and vans to take people on day-tours to the snowfields. Each coach that goes has exactly 41 people and each van has exactly 9 people. If 304 people go to the snowfields with the tour company, how many vans were used?

Q6. A construction contractor has tow types of ladder, viz: - short ladders with 5 rungs and long ladders with 8 rungs. It total there are 123 rungs. If the contractor has more long ladders than short ladders, how many long ladders are there?

Q7. Senior bricklayers can lay 95 bricks per hour and juniors 52 bricks per hour. In one hour 545 bricks were laid. How many senior and junior bricklayers were employed?

Q8. Pre-mixed concrete can be transported to a major construction site by "Monster" or "Convoy" trucking firms. "Monster" trucks have a capacity of 23 m and cost $400 per trip. "Convoy" trucks hold 18 m and cost $300 per trip. What is the cheapest method of conveying 1000m of pre-mixed concrete to a construction site?

9. A shop in Busselton (WA) sells two types of tourist maps : winery maps for $1.10 each and forestry maps for $1.70 each. At the start of one day it had 29 maps in stock. Its sales for the day were $37.40, after selling more than one of each type of map . What was the total number of maps sold?

10. A school bought 35 calculators for sale to students. One brand sold for $13 each and the other brand for $17 each. Total sales from these two brands were $534. What was the total number of calculators sold?

11. Lasagne costs $7 and Ravioli $5 at a lunch cafe. A number of people in a group had one meal each and had to choose one or the other, spending a total of $74. More people had Lasagne than Ravioli. How many had Lasagne?

12. A stationery supplier wishes to market pads in large bundles of 15 and small bundles of 7. His clerical staff deliver 175 loose pads and the supplier has to make them into some bundles of each type so that none are left over. How many small bundles does the stationery supplier form?

13. Our local bakery sells cookies in large packets of 11 and small packets of 7. It had 276 loose cookies and wanted to put them into packets without any wastage, and with more large than small packets. How many large packets did the bakery make?

DIOPHANTINE EQUATIONS

14. Railway shunters in Brisbane have to arrange 98 carriages into large trains with 11 carriages each and small trains with 5 carriages each, with more small trains needed than large ones. How many of each type should the shunters arrange so that no carriages remain?

15. A company sells a spray to farmers in large containers of 40 L and small ones of 9 L. How can it allocate 334 L of the spray without wastage?

16. The hardware manager has to put 224 bolts into large boxes of 19 and small boxes of 3. He uses more large boxes than small boxes. How many boxes of each type should the manager form?

17. A retired man makes toy cars and tricycles for a hobby. Each type of toy uses the same wheels. He has to make at least 2 of each type and decides to make more cars than tricycles. If he uses exactly 43 wheels, how many of each type of toy does he make?

18. A pet shop takes $142 in a day by selling parrots for $7 each and canaries for $5 each. If the shop had only 25 birds in stock in total and sold more canaries than parrots, how many parrots were sold?

Q19. In a big garage there are twelve buses, some with 4 wheels and some with 6 wheels. If there are 58 wheels in total, how many small (4 wheeled) buses are there?

Q20. A school bought 35 calculators for sale to students. Brand X sold for $13 each and Brand Y for $17 each. A total of $522 was collected. How many calculators were sold?

Q21. The local bakery sorted all of its 263 muffins into some packs of 14 and other packs of 15. How many packs of each type was that?

Q22. Tennis balls are packed in cylinders of 3 balls or cubic boxes of 7 balls. The sporting goods factory has 104 balls to pack, and needs to pack more cubic boxes than cylinders, but must have at least 3 cylinders. How many of each type of pack should the factory arrange without any "leftover" tennis balls?

Q23. Red roses sell for $3 each and yellow ones for $5 each. The total sales for the florist on the two types of roses was $98, with more yellow ones being sold than red ones. One person bought 7 red ones. How many of each type were sold?

Q24. The lighting specialist has 2 products: the "Gleaner" which sells for $23 each and the Standard light fitting that sells for $13 each. One day its total sales were $373. How many of each were sold?

MATHEMATICAL WORD PROBLEMS

Q25. One hot day, Darren buys some bottles of orange drink, which cost 85¢ per bottle, and lime drink which cost 95¢ per bottle, spending a total of $6.35. How many of each type did he buy?

Q26. In Australian Rules, a team scores 6 points for a goal and 1 point for a behind. If a team has 27 points and has scored more goals than behinds, how many goals has it scored?

Q27. A garden centre sells Roses for $7 each and Camellias for $8. If a customer bought at least one of each type of plant and spent a total of $96, how many of each type of plant did she buy?

Q28. A gardener uses a fertiliser on roses and camellias. Each rose needs 5 units and each camellia 7 units of the fertiliser. The gardener in meeting the needs of all her plants uses 139 units of fertiliser. How many of each type of plant does she apply the fertiliser to, given that she applied it to more than twice as many camellias as roses?

Q29. Membership of a flower club cost $2 for adults and 50¢ for pensioners. Total membership contributions are $55. There are a majority of pensioners in the club and less that 50 people in total. How many pensioners are in the club?

Q30. A pet shop sells rabbits for $5 each and canaries for $7 each. In a certain days trading, it took $97 and sold more canaries than rabbits. Find the number of each type of pet it sold.

Q31. A trader at the football sells two types of beanies: Raiders baenies for $7 each and plain ones for $5 each. His total receipts from sales is $74. The trader sold more Raiders beanies than plain beanies. How many Raiders beanies did the trader sell?

Q32. I wish to buy 100 animals. Cats cost me $5 each, rabbits $1 and fish 5¢ each. I have $100 to spend and buy at least one of each animal. If I spent all of my money on the purchase of these animals, how many of each kind of animal did I buy?

Q33. A person buys a total of 100 blocks of chocolate. The blocks are available in three sizes, some cost 35¢ each. others 40¢ for three and others 5¢ each. If the total cost is $10, how many blocks of each size does the person buy? (3 possible solutions).

Q34. The confectionary shop sorted all of its 174 toffees into bags of 10 and 21. How many bags of each type was that?

DIOPHANTINE EQUATIONS

Q35. A factory makes baby tricycles (3 wheels) and toy cars (4 wheels). It must make more tricycles than cars, abut can only produce a total of at most 24 such toy vehicles in a day. The wheels are common to both types of vehicles. If, in a day, the factory used 83 wheels, how many tricycles did it make?

Q36. At a wildlife park the kangaroos eat 40 units of protein per day; the Tasmanian devils eat 65 units of protein per day; while the possums only eat 2 units of protein per day. The wildlife part uses 3279 units of protein each day feeding 100 of these types of animals. How many kangaroos are in the wildlife park?

Q37. A stall at the baseball took a total of $381 by selling straw hats for $11 each and felt hats for $15 each. More straw hats than felt hats were sold. How many of each style were sold?

Q38. A single train journey from Sydney to Auburn costs $2, from Sydney to Blacktown costs $4 and from Sydney to Penrith costs $5. These are the only 3 stops. If 100 passengers paid a total of $210 how many went from Sydney to Auburn?(assume at least 1 person got off at each stop).

Q39. At McGrath's Hill Sale only pigs, sheep and chickens were sold. Pigs cost $6 each, sheep $8 each and chickens 50¢ each. I bought 100 animals for $100. How many of each animal did I buy?

Q40. A trader at the football sells caps for $21 each and jumpers for $55 each, taking a total of $338. How many caps and jumpers did the trader sell?

Q41. Berrima Silversmiths charge 50¢ each for cleaning teaspoons, $3 each for cleaning goblets and $6 each for cleaning trophies. Mrs Dempster took at least one of each of these items to Berrima Silversmiths and in the total spent $100 having 100 items cleaned. How many of each item did Mrs Dempster have cleaned?

Q42. Wendy planted a 50 m long flower bed with Pansies, Begonias and Carnations. Pansies cost $9 per metre to plant, Begonias $2 per metre and Carnations $3 per metre. Wendy planted at least 2 metres of each type of plant. If she spent $120 in total, how many metres of each type did she plant, given that she planted an integral number of metres of each type ?

Q43. If you purchased 3 pair of discount socks and 7 pairs of fashion socks for a cost of $78 and fashion socks cost more than discount socks, what is the price (in whole numbers of dollars) of each type of socks?

MATHEMATICAL WORD PROBLEMS

Q44. At Gunnedah saleyards a farmer paid a total of $650 for lambs which cost $10 each and calves which cost $17 each. The farmer bought more calves than lambs. How many of each type of animal did the farmer buy?

Q45. Louis the barber takes 7 minutes to cut a man's hair and 5 minutes to cut a boy's hair. Had he worked without stopping (ignore changeover time) for 41 minutes, how many men and boys did he give a haircut?

Q46. On a pipeline construction job, Jimmy the welder takes 6 minutes to install a valve and 11 minutes to install a pump. If he works non-stop for one and a quarter hours (ignore changeover times) how many pumps and valves does he install?

Q47. Justin and Clare pick cherries from the tree in their backyard and put them into plastic packets to give to their friends at school. Justin puts 6 cherries into each of his packets and Clare puts 11 cherries into each of her packets. Clare had more packets than Justin to take to school. If they picked a total of 164 cherries, how many packets did each child pick and pack?

Q48. Danny fixes furniture. One day he fixed only tables and chairs and earned a total of $106. He fixed more tables than chairs. He charges $5 each to fix chairs and $7 each to fix tables. How many of each did he fix on that day?

Q49. Lachlan Hot Air Balloons has two balloons Wasp and Eagle. Wasp can carry 7 passengers and Eagle can carry 10. Balloons only leave when there are enough passengers to equal carrying capacity. One day the company carried a total of 92 passengers. How many trips did each balloon make?

Q50. Linda went to the garden centre and bought some red camellias bushes for $3 each and white camellias bushes for $5 each. She bought more than 2 of each type and bought more white ones than red ones, spending a total of $53. How many of each type did she buy?

Q51. Riverstone Sports Club awards gold and red pennants (ie cotton flags) to its successful members. Each gold pennant has an area of 25 cm² while each red one has an area of 18 cm². If a total of 337 cm² was used making the pennants, how many of each type was awarded to members?

Q52. Mrs Harvey teaches children to play the xylophone. Some of these have 7 keys and others have 8 keys. In total all the xylophones she uses have a total of 68 keys. How many of each type does she have?

DIOPHANTINE EQUATIONS

Q53. Sam's Sawdust delivers sawdust to the racetrack in trailers, some of which carry 11m² and others 9 m². He delivers more than 3 trailer loads using each type of trailer. If he delivers 184 m² of sawdust how many trailer loads of each type does he deliver?

Q54. Carl's Coaches uses two types of coaches for its day tours. One type can seat 19 passengers and the other type 15 passengers. If the total capacity of Carl's fleet is 298 seats, how many of each coach does Carl have?

Q55. The merry-go-round in the shopping centre charges $2 for a ride on a pony and $3 for a ride on an elephant. Caroline had at least on ride of each type of animal costing her parents $14. She went on more pony rides than elephant rides. How many rides of each type of animal did Caroline have?

Q56. Tom's Tanbark delivered 142 m³ of tanbark to the municipal gardens. Tom used 3 different types of trailers of capacity 5 m³, 7 m³ and 11 m³. He used twice as many 7 m³ loads than 5 m³ loads. How many of each type of trailer did Tom use?

Q57. A class is given yoghurt in small tubs, some of which contain 5 g of fat, others, the low-fat style contain 2 g of fat. In total the class consumed 71 g of fat, with more of the low-fat variety being consumed. If there were less than 24 tubs given out in total how many of each type were consumed?

Q58. A wildlife park keeps emus and wombats, having more than 6 of each. Emus need 7 units of food each per day and wombats 11. If the wildlife park uses 151 units of food per day, how many emus and wombats are there in the park?

Q59. A wildlife park charges adults $9 and children $5 for admission. One afternoon the total admission money raised was $468. More than 20 children attended and there were more adults than children. How many adults and children attended?

Q60. The local club charges $7 for members and $9 for visitors to have a meal. On a particular night there are at least 40 patrons of each type having a meal with more members than visitors. On this night gross takings were $816. How many members and visitors had a meal on this night?

Q61. Mrs Hill bought a number of packets of washing powder some with a net weight of 1.5 kg, the rest with a net weight of 2 kg. In total the net weight of washing powder she bought was 34 kg. She bought more than 6 packets of each size and bought more 2 kg packets than 1.5 kg packets. How many of each sized packet did she buy?

MATHEMATICAL WORD PROBLEMS

Q62. Mr Jess takes people on tours to various cities in South America by air. There are two types of tours: Rio Grande in which he flies into 8 cities and Aztec in which he flies into 11 cities. In a year he made 111 landings at the airports in these cities. How many of each type of tour did he take in that year?

Q63. The Blacktown Baseball Club sent one of its members out to buy fried chicken pieces. He had a choice of packs between: Single packs with 3 pieces; Dinky packs with 4 pieces; Family packs with 7 pieces. He bought at least 10 of each type of pack with more Family Packs than Dinky Packs. If he returned to the Club with 158 pieces of chicken in total, how many of each type of pack did he buy?

Q64. Robin bought a number of cans of ironing spray, some of which had net contents of 300 g and the rest with net contents of 500 g. She bought more of the smaller cans than the larger cans, giving her a total net amount of 3.6 kg of ironing spray. How many of each size can did she buy?

Q65. Two building groups construct a number of nursing homes for elderly people in a given region. Company A builds nursing homes that each cater for 27 residents, while Company B builds nursing homes that each cater for 37 residents. In total 468 elderly residents area catered for. How many nursing homes did each company build?

Q66. On a small dairy farm each Jersey cow produces 7 litres of milk and each Friesian cow produces 11 litres of milk in a day. The dairy farm has more Friesian cows than Jersey cows and at least 5 of each type. If 245 litres of milk is the daily output, how many of each type of cow is on the dairy farm?

Q67. Soap is sold in packets of 3 and 4 cakes in the supermarket. Mandy buys a number of packets of each type giving her 46 cakes of soap in total. She bought more 4-cake packets than 3-cake packets. If she bought at least 3 of each type, how many of each type did she buy?

Q68. A small factory makes 2 types of jigsaw puzzles, the Dolphin has 23 pieces and the Galah has 13 pieces. One day it used 362 pieces in total without any wastage. How many Dolphin jigsaw puzzles did it make?

Q69. Julie bought some old CD's for $3 each and new CD's for $19 each, spending a total of $116. The total number of CD's she bought was more than 15. How many old CD's did Julie buy?

Q70. A cabinet maker has 49 table legs which he use to make 3-legged and 4-legged tables. He makes more 4-legged tables than 3 legged tables. How many of each does he make?

DIOPHANTINE EQUATIONS

Q71. An electronic company has a contract with a school to repair Data Projectors for $17 each and Camcorders for $30 each. If one day's work it charged the school $175, how many of each type of appliance did the company repair?

Q72. A tour company uses coaches and vans to take people on day-tours to the snowfields. Each coach that goes has exactly 41 people and each van has exactly 9 people. If 222 people go to the snowfields with the tour company, how many vans were used?

Q73. A construction contractor has two types of ladders, viz short ladders with 5 rungs and long ladders with 9 rungs. In total there are 134 rungs. If the contractor has more long ladders than short ladders, how many long ladders are there?

Q74. Senior bricklayers can lay 75 bricks per hour and juniors 46 bricks per hour. In one hour 455 bricks were laid. How many senior and junior bricklayers were employed?

Q75. A fried chicken outlet sells only Budget packs each containing 3 pieces of chicken and Family packs each containing 19 pieces of chicken. It always sells more Family packs than Budget packs. One evening it sold a total of 224 pieces of chicken. How many Family packs did the outlet sell on that evening?

Q76. A factory makes two types of surfboards. "Moppy" which use 5L of wax-coating and "Gummy: which use 6L of wax-coating. It must make more "Moppy" boards than "Gummy" boards, but must make at least 9 "Gummy" boards per week. In all it used 163L of wax-coating in a week. How many of each brand did it make?

Q77. The veterinary surgeon charges $17 to treat each dog and $37 to treat each horse when visiting a stud farm. If the bill for a visit was $361 how many dogs and horses were treated?

Q78. The local hot bread shop sorted all its 227 bread rolls into some bags of 12 and some bags of 13. How many bags of each number were there?

Q79. A fast food chain gives away to children 183 colouring pencils in small boxes of 7 each and large boxes of 17 each. How many small and large boxes were used?

Q80 A souvenir shop sells maps for $6 each and hats for $35 each, taking a total of $112 from the sale of the two types of product. How many of each did the shop sell?

Q81. A stall at the markets gets its apples from Batlow and puts them into small bags of 7 and large bags of 17. How can 281 apples be sorted this way to minimise the number of bags used?

MATHEMATICAL WORD PROBLEMS

Q82. Bridget spent $15 buying 15 items from the cake shop. She bought some donuts for 25 cents each, some finger buns for 50 cents each and some fruit pies for $3 each. How many fruit pies did she buy?

Q83. The students of Year 10 put on a play at which 120 people attended paying a total of $120. Parents paid $2 each, students 10 cents each and visitors paid $5 each. How many parents, students and visitors attended the play?

ANSWERS

1.

1. 11
2. 20 cards, 17 stamps, 13 notebooks
3. 3 x 3-legged tables; 9 x 4-legged tables
4. 5 data projectors and 3 camcorders
5. 11
6. 11
7. 3 seniors; 5 juniors
8. 53 Convoys; 2 Monsters
9. 28
10. 34
11. 7
12. 10
13. 20
14. 3 large, 13 small
15. 7 large and 6 small
16. 11 large, 5 small
17. 7 cars and 5 tricycles
18. 11 parrots
19. 7
20. 34
21. 7 packs of 14 muffins each and 11 packs of 15 muffins each
22. 9 cylinders and 11 cubic boxes
23. 11 red, 13 yellow
24. 10 Gleaner and 11 standard
25. 3 bottles of orange drink and 4 lime drinks
26. 4 goals
27. 8 roses and 5 camellias
28. 17 camellias, 4 roses
29. 26
30. 4 rabbits, 11 canaries
31. 7
32. 19 cats, 1 rabbit, 80 fish
33. 3 possible answers; 5 x 35¢, 42 x 40¢, 53 x 5¢; / 10 x 35¢, 24 x 40¢, 66 x 5¢ 15 x 35¢, 6 x 40¢, 79 x 5¢.
34. 9 bags of 10 toffees each and 4 bags of 21 toffees each
35. 13
36. 23
37. 21 straw and 10 felt
38. 96

39. 5 pigs, 3 sheep, 92 chickens
40. 3 caps and 5 jumpers
41. 86 teaspoons, 9 goblets, 5 trophies
42. 2m pansies; 42m begonias, 6m carnations
43. Discount $5 per pair, Fashion $9 per pair
44. 30 calves and 14 lambs
45. 3 men and 4 boys
46. 7 valves and 3 pumps
47. Justin 9 packets; Clare 10 packets
48. 3 chairs and 13 tables
49. Wasp 6 trips; and Eagle 5 trips
50. 6 red, 7 white
51. 7 gold, 9 red
52. 4 x 7 keys; 5 x 8 keys
53. 7 x 9m^2, 11 x 11m^2
54. 7 x 19 seaters; 11 x 15 seaters
55. 4 pony rides; 2 elephant rides
56. 4 x 5m^3, 8 x 7m^3, 6 x 11m^3
57. 9 x 5g variety; 13 x 2g low fat variety
58. 9 emus; 8 wombats
59. 37 adults, 27 children
60. 60 members; 44 visitors
61. 8 x 1.5 kg; 11 x 2 kg
62. Rio Grande 7 tours; Aztec 5 tours
63. Single 10; Dinky 11; Family 12
64. 7 x 300g; 3 x 500g
65. A 5; B 9
66. Jersey 13; Friesian 14
67. 6, 7
68. 5
69. 26
70. 3 x 3-legged tables, 10 x 4-legged tables
71. 5 Data projectors and 3 camcorders
72. 11
73. 11
74. 3 seniors and 5 juniors
75. 11
76. Moppy 17, Gummy 13
77. 6 dogs and 7 horses
78. 7 bags of 12 rolls each and 11 bags of 13 rolls each
79. 14 small boxes and 5 large boxes
80. 7 maps and 2 hats
81. 11 bags of 7 apples each and 12 bags of 17 apples each. NB there is another answer 28, 5 but this involves using 10 extra bags.
82. 4 fruit pies
83. 17 visitors, 13 parents, 90 students

Ω
MISCELLANEOUS AND SPECIALS

Q1. My dog is sick. The vet gave me pills to give my dog and said a pill could not be taken more than once in any period of less than 1 hour, and also that the dog could not be given more than 6 in any period of 12 hours. What is the largest number of pills I can give my dog between 5 am and 11 pm on the same day?

Q2. Eight years ago my father was 3 times as old as I shall be in 5 years time. He was 41 years old when I was born. How old am I now?

Q3. Four tennis players decide to redistribute the prize money they won during the season. Andre doubled Boris' money - in other words he gave Boris as much money as he had. Then Boris doubled Roy's money, then Roy doubled Pancho's money and finally Pancho doubled Andre's money. Then they each had $16000. How much did each start with?

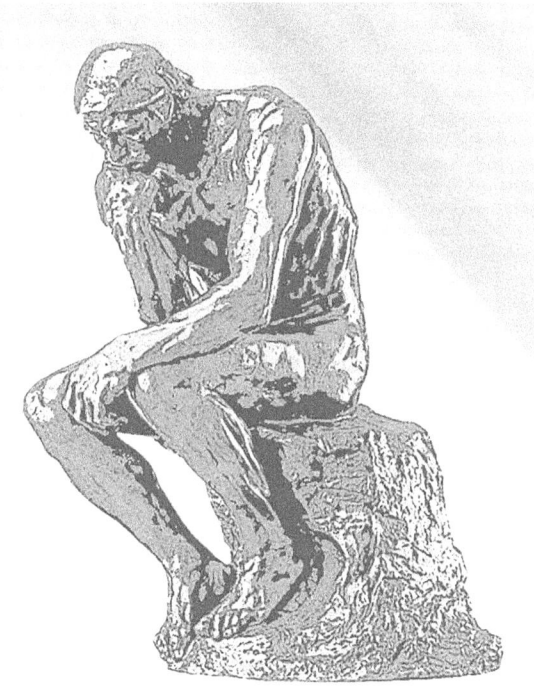

MATHEMATICAL WORD PROBLEMS

Q4. Two mosquito coils "Repello" and "Duro" have different lengths and different thicknesses. "Duro" can burn for 10 hours and "Repello" for 7 hours. Duro is the shorter of the two. After 4 hours burning both coils have the same length. Find the ratio of the length of the "Duro" to the length of "Repello".

Q5. The units digit of a 2 digit number is 1. If the order of the digits was reversed, the new number obtained would be 36 less than the original number. What is the number?

Q6. The escalators at Central Station have 54 steps visible at any one time. Terry runs twice as quickly as Lorraine walks. Terry goes up 36 steps before reaching the top. How many steps has Lorraine climbed before she gets to the top?

Q7. There are three sisters Marie, Christine and Patricia. Marie is as old as Patricia and Christine together. Last year Patricia was twice as old as Christine. In two years time Marie will be twice as old as Christine. What are the current ages of the 3 girls?

Q8. An unpainted wooden cube is painted green on all its faces. It is then cut into 27 equal smaller cubes. How many of these smaller cubes are painted green on (a) 3 faces; (b) 1 face; (c) no faces.

Q9. If a passenger train and goods train pass in opposite directions, it takes a certain time for them to pass each other. However, if they were going in the same direction, it would take the passenger train twice as long (ie. twice this certain time) to pass the goods train after first overtaking it. How many times faster than the goods train is the passenger train?

Q10. Mrs Ducrow, Mrs Adams and Mrs Robb, whose first names are Maureen, Christine and Wendy, not necessarily in that order, went shopping one day. Wendy spent twice as much as Christine and Christine spent three times as much as Maureen. Mrs Ducrow spent $3.85 more than Mrs Robb. What is each woman's full name?

Q11. Grandad is aged between 65 and 100 and claims that if the digits in his age multiplied, the result would be equal to his age 40 years ago. How old is Grandad?

Q12. Two spheres of diameter 6 cm and 4 cm resting on a horizontal table touch each other at A. How high is A above the table?

Q13. A boy in high school has 9 different books, two for mathematics, and one each for his other 7 subjects. In how many different ways can these 9 books be arranged on a shelf so that the two mathematics books are next to each other?

MISCELLANEOUS AND SPECIALS

Q14. A piece of plastic pipe 60 cm long is cut into 2 parts in the ratio 2:1. Each part is then bent to for a square. What is the total area of the two squares?

Q15. Mr Hanish, a scientist, loves riding his big motorcycle in the country. One day he noticed his odometer read the same backwards as forwards. In other words the total distance his motorcycle had travelled was 15951 kms. How many more kilometres will Mr Hanish have to ride his motorcycle before the odometer again (next) shows a number that reads the same backwards as forwards.

Q16. Justin and Clare's ages add up to 25. Clare and Dominic's ages add up to 29. Caroline is 14. Her age is exactly half way between Justin's and Dominic's ages. How old is everyone?

Q17. A computer competition awarded 19 prizes to students from country areas. The total value of all prizes was $1000. Each student from a farm was to receive so many dollars exactly, and each student from the towns was to receive $30 more than each student from a farm. After a debate it was decided this was unfair and as a result each student from a farm was awarded $8 more than the original idea stated above. Prizes awarded to students from the towns were scaled down accordingly. How much did each category of student received?

Q18. Every hour on the hour, beginning at midnight, a coach leaves Gunnedah for Cowra, a distance of 301 kms. At the same time, a coach leaves Cowra for Gunnedah - ie on the hour every hour. Every coach travels at a constant speed of 60 kph. Suppose a particular coach leaves from Gunnedah at 7 am on its way to Cowra. How many coaches will this coach meet on its way to Cowra?

Q19. The lengths of the diagonals of a rectangular block of land plus the lengths of its longer sides, are together equal to seven times one of the shorter sides. Also the length of one diagonal is 250 m longer than the length of one of the shorter sides. What is the area of the rectangular block of land?

Q20. Mrs Moylan is teaching her class a counting game. After taking 2 steps forward, they must take one step backward. Using this rule, what is the least number of steps a student in her class must take in order to reach the school gate which is 7 steps away?

Q21. In a rectangle, the shorter side is four times the difference between the diagonal and the longer side. Find the ratio of the longer side to the shorter side.

Q22. In a school of 405 pupils a survey on sporting activities shows that 251 pupils play tennis, 157 play hockey and 111 play softball. There are 45 pupils who play both tennis and hockey, 60 who play hockey and softball and 39 who play tennis and softball. What conclusion may be drawn about the number of those who participate in all three sports?

Q23. Some bush-walkers set out at 10 am and return on the same track to their starting point at 4 pm. If their speed is 4 km per hour on level ground, 3 km an hour uphill and 6 km per hour downhill, how far do they walk?

Q24. A bus takes thirty minutes to travel (non-stop) the distance between two terminals. Buses leave one terminal regularly at ten-minute intervals and travel uniformly, all at the same speed. A car leaves the terminal simultaneously with one of the buses, and travels to the other terminal at four times the speed of the buses. How many buses will the car overtake by the time it reaches the terminus?

Q25. There were two bricklayers Con and Terry. Con on his own could build a certain wall in 9 hours, while Terry, on his own, could build the same wall in 10 hours. If they worked together, because they joked a lot, 10 fewer bricks got laid per hour. They finally got the job of building this wall and did the job in 5 hours. How many bricks were in the wall?

Q26. The year 1961 had the rare property of reading the same upside down. Excluding the year zero, how many years (AD) has this been true, and how long will it be before it occurs again?

Q27. Suppose 100 singers have to perform at a concert in such a way that each singer performs only once. Further, each act must contain a different number of singers ie only one solo, only one duet etc....What is the largest number of acts that the concert can contain?

Q28. Emily walks to school each morning. when she has walked a quarter of the way she passes the cake shop; when she has walked one third of the way she passes the swimming pool. The clock on the wall at the cake shop shows 7.30 am, and the clock at the swimming pool shows 7.35 am. When does Emily get to school?

Q29. A clock is set correctly at 1 pm and then loses 3 minutes every hour. The next day when the correct time is 10 am, what will the clock read?

Q30. Farmer Davis has two water tanks which he calls "Big" and "Small". At midday, when each tank was full, Farmer Davis used a pump to draw water from each tank at a constant, though not necessarily equal, rate. At 2 pm the tanks had the same depth of water. "Big" tank ran dry at 5 pm. "Small" tank, which is 10 metres high, ran dry at 8 pm. How high is "Big" tank?

MISCELLANEOUS AND SPECIALS

Q31. In her kindergarten class, Rebecca was writing out the numbers starting from 1. Suddenly the teacher asked the class to stop and count how many <u>digits</u> they had written. Rebecca had written 288 digits. What was the last number Rebecca had written?

Q32. A mining company has to use its vehicles on very rough ground. The front tyres last 25 000 kms while the back tyres last only 15 000 kms. After a number of kilometres the front and back tyres are interchanged. What is the maximum distance a vehicle can be driven without using new tyres?

Q33. The transport inspectors in the outback have cars that have front tyres that last 56 000 kms and back tyres that last 42 000 kms. After a number of kilometres the front and back tyres are interchanged. What is the maximum distance a vehicle can be driven without using new tyres?

Q34. Tim the angry football coach is going to drop any player from his team who arrives at training after 6 pm. Laurie's watch is 10 minutes fast but he thinks it is 5 minutes slow. Ossie's watch is 5 minutes fast but he thinks it is 10 minutes slow. Mal's watch is 10 minutes slow but he thinks it is 10 minutes fast. Badge's watch is 5 minute slow but he thinks it is 10 minutes fast. All four of these players using their watches leave in what he believes is time to get to training by 6 pm. Which two players does Tim drop from the team?

Q35. Ken is 160 metres ahead of Gerard in the steeplechase, but Gerard is catching up. For every 7 metres Ken runs, Gerard runs 9 metres. How many more metres will Gerard have to run to catch up to Ken?

Q36. Cliff and Spiro take part in a marathon race from Katoomba to Lithgow. They have only one horse between them. Cliff rides for a while and then ties up the horse for Spiro who has been jogging. Cliff then jogs ahead. They keep doing this alternatively jogging and riding. If they jog at 4 km per hour and ride the horse at 12 km per hour, what part of the time is the horse resting?

Q37. (a) Carl has 4 students in his music class learning to play trumpet. Each one goes home putting their trumpet into the wrong case. In other words each came away with one of the other 3 students trumpet cases. In how many different ways could this have been done?

(b) Diana has 5 students who all make the same mistake as Carl's 4 students in part (a). In how many different ways could this happen?

MATHEMATICAL WORD PROBLEMS

Q38. Ink spilt on an account at Brown Tower Cafe so that the auditor could only read part of it. All she could see was: 45 bottles of wine at $5 * # each = $2*4.3*. Four digits could not be read. What was the full statement?

Q39. Lauren is a little girl who walks along the footpath to kindergarten, normally taking two paces (strides) to each uniform concrete slab. If she increases her pace (stride) by 6 cms she takes 5 strikes to each 3 concrete slabs. What is the length of her normal stride?

Q40. Dione and Tammy played chess one night. To make matters interesting they play for chocolates, the loser handing over one at the end of each game. There are no ties. (drawn games). During the course of the night one girl won a net total of 10 chocolates from the other. When the nigh ended they each had 6 chocolates, although Tammy had eater 3 and Dione 7 during the night's play. How many chocolates did Tammy have at the start of the night's play?

Q41. The paediatrician saw 6 children today and wrote down their ages (in whole numbered years) on a sheet of paper. The product of all their ages was 30030 and the sum of all their ages was 41. How old were the 6 children?

Q42. In the Belconnen markets all the oranges are the same shape (spherical) and size. They are stacked in triangular pyramids. Each layer (Level) of oranges forms the shape of an equilateral triangle. The top layer is just one single orange. The second layer contains three oranges. How many oranges are there in a stack that is 10 layers high?

Q43. Friday the 13th day of any month is considered with superstition in many cultures. What is the least and greatest number of times Friday 13th (or the 13th day of any month is a Friday) can fall in any one calendar year?

Q44. A billiard table measures 3 m by 2 m internally from cushion to cushion. A ball is struck so that it rebounds off all 4 sides and returns precisely to its original position. Find the total distance travelled by the ball.

Q45. The students in Year 10 had to answer 2 questions in a short test. Both questions were answered correctly by 37 of the students. A third of the students were wrong on Question 1, and a quarter of them were wrong on Question 2. A fifth of the students got both questions wrong. How many students sat the test?

Q46. Cliff is a retired marathon runner who would not say his age. He said "If you reverse the digits on my age, you'll get half of what I will be in a year's time." How old is Cliff?

MISCELLANEOUS AND SPECIALS

Q47. Three girls Carmen, Natasha and Leanne catch the train at Mulgrave Station to go to school. One of the girls belongs to Little Athletics, another is a swimmer while the third belongs to Windsor Hockey Club. They are in a rock band together, each playing a different instrument. One plays the guitar, one the clarinet and one the drums. Leanne lives halfway between the drummer and the girl in the Little Athletics. Carmen and the girl in Little Athletics are cousins. Natasha and the clarinet player go to different churches on Sunday. What instrument do each of the girls play?

Q48. A tourist coach took 24 visitors to a lunch where the cost was a fixed amount of money somewhere between $9.70 and $9.90 each no matter how much food was eaten. When the bill arrived it stated "24 lunches $23*.3*. Two of the digits were obscured. What were the two digits, and hence what was the total?

Q49. A transport company has a contract to take 21 identical cylinders in 3 trucks from Botany to Forbes. The cylinders must arrive in Forbes unopened. Seven of the cylinders are empty, seven are filled with a toxic chemical, and the other seven are half-filled with the toxic chemical. The three truck drivers Terry, Green-Dog and Slim insist that the total weight is equally distributed between the 3 trucks. Devise two ways that the demands of the drivers could be met.

Q50. Newcastle and Canberra are 450 km apart. Mr Cave travels from Newcastle to Canberra at a uniform speed of 55 kph. Mrs Drynan travels from Canberra to Newcastle at a uniform speed of 60 kph. They leave at exactly half past the hour (not necessarily at the same time). They meet at exactly half past an hour. How far has Mrs Drynan travelled when they meet?

Q51. Find the three digit number such that is you subtract 7 from it the result is divisible by 7; if you subtract 8 from it the result is divisible by 8, and if you subtract 9 from it the result is divisible by 9

Q52. Two mosquito coils of the same length and thickness are lit at 7 pm. After 4 hours one coil burns out, but the other lasts for another hour before is too, is burnt out. What time was it when one coil was twice the length of the other?

Q53. The local council decided to plant 10 different trees in a park. They has 6 different types of pine trees, 5 different species of gum trees and 4 different species of poplar trees to select the 10 trees from. If the Mayor insisted that there be at least 3 pine trees, 3 gum trees and 3 poplars, in how many ways can the 10 trees be planted?

MATHEMATICAL WORD PROBLEMS

Q54. A committee has to be formed of 2 people each from Tasmania, Victoria and Queensland. If there were 5 people from Tasmania, 4 from Victoria and 3 from Queensland applying to be on this committee, in how many ways can the committee be made up?

Q55. Three candidates Fahey, Carr and Goss stood for an election. Fahey received 9500 votes. Carr and Fahey obtained 75% of the votes between them. Carr and Goss together polled 17 500 votes. How many votes did Goss receive?

Q56. I drove from Lithgow to Dubbo via Orange. After one hour car trouble at Orange forced me to slow down to $\frac{2}{3}$ of my original speed. I reached Dubbo 2 hours later than I had planned. Had my car trouble occurred 50 kilometres past Orange, I would have arrived 30 minutes earlier than I actually did arrive. What is the distance from Lithgow to Dubbo?

Q57. The Woods family are an extended family who went to pick cherries in Young (NSW) one day. There are more women than men and more men than children in the Woods family. Each member of the family was given a target number of boxes of cherries to pick. The targets were such that 2 men picked as many boxes as 3 women and 2 children, while 5 women picked as many boxes as 3 men and 1 child. All targets were in whole numbers, each person had to pick as many boxes as everyone else in his or her category and 116 boxes were picked in total. How many men, women and children are there in the Woods family.

Q58. Peter went to pay his credit card bill by cheque but wrote his cheque incorrectly, getting the dollars and cents mixed up. The cashier looked at Peter and said "That's not enough Peter, your bill was between $52 and $53 and you have made the cheque out the wrong way around" Peter then gave the cashier a cash amount. The cashier said "That's still not enough Peter, you have to give me double that amount of cash on top of what you have already paid to get things right; you still owe me between $10 and $11." Peter then gave the cashier more cash and his credit card bill was fully paid. What was Peter's original bill?

Q59. Last week Aunt Mary packed up her possessions in order to move into a retirement village in Katoomba. While doing so she found some old notes, some $1, some $5 and some $10 hidden in a tin under the house. There was at least 1 of each type of note and their total value was $199. There were less than 25 notes in total. How many of each type of note did she find?

MISCELLANEOUS AND SPECIALS

Q60. Mrs Renouf was moving house and hired Clumsy Convoy to carry her belongings. Clumsy Convoy had a minor accident and all her glasses broke. Mrs Renouf did not remember how many glasses she had but knew that when she divided the number by 2,3,4,5 or 6 there was always 1 glass left over. If the glasses had been packed in groups of 7 there would have been an integral number of packs (ie. none left over). What is the least number of glasses broken by Clumsy Convoy's accident?

Q61. Merici College sold 2 000 raffle tickets in books of 5, numbered 1 to 5, 6 to 10, 11 to 15, and so on up to the last book whose tickets were numbered 1996 to 2000. The winning ticket was the middle one in one of those books. When the Maths teachers at Merici College added up the 5 ticket numbers in that book that contained the winning ticket, they noticed that the answer had each of the ten numbers: 1,2,3,4,5,6,7,8,9,10 as factors. What was the number of the winning ticket?

Q62. The Australian Mathematics Trust wanted to book 4 rooms at a resort in Darwin for a conference. The room numbers start from 2 and go up to 750. When the people from the Trust arrived in Darwin the receptionist told them "Your room numbers are all perfect cubes and three of them add up to the fourth." What were the numbers of the rooms allocated to the Trust?

Q63. A cow and a goat would eat all the grass in a paddock in 50 days. A goat and a lamb would eat all the grass in the same paddock in 75 days. A cow and a lamb would eat all the grass in the same paddock in 60 days. How long would the grass in this paddock last if a cow, a goat and a lamb were to eat there together?

Q64. The manager of a factory making hats decides to give some stock away to some or all of the staff. If he gives 7 hats each to the few staff in the storeroom there will be none left over. If he gives all the staff 2 hats each there will be 2 left over. If he gives the staff in the storeroom and the cutting room 3 hats each there will be 3 hats left over. What is the smallest number of hats to be given away?

Q65. One day Toby was writing all the numbers from 1 to 300 in order but was disturbed by a phone call part way through the process. At that point he had written a total of 291 digits. What was the last number he had written?

Q66. During the month of May, three members of the Gonzales Family, Maria, Jose and Ernesto each did 777 mathematics problems. Each wrote down the number he/she got wrong, each number being greater than 1. When these numbers were multiplied together the product was 777. If Ernesto got the most wrong and Maria the least, how many did each get wrong?

ANSWERS

1. 12
2. 9 years old
3. Andre $23 000, Boris $15 000, Roy $14 000 and Pancho $12 000.
4. 5:7
5. 51
6. 27
7. Marie is 8, Christine 3, Patricia 5
8. 8 are painted green on 3 faces; 6 are painted green on 1 face; only 1 face is not painted green
9. The passenger train is three times as fast as the goods train
10. Wendy Ducrow; Christine Adams; Maureen Robb
11. 75
12. 2.4 cm
13. 80 640
14. 125 cm^2
15. 110 kms (NB - a number like 15951 or 48384 is called palindrome)
16. Caroline is 14; Justin is 12; Clare is 13; Dominic is 16
17. Town students get $59 each; Farm students get $48 each
18. 11
19. 126 000 m^2
20. 17 steps
21. 15:8
22. ≤12 take all 3 sports.
23. 24 km
24. 3 buses (including the one at the start)
25. 900
26. 23 times it has happened but it won't happen again until the year 6009
27. 13
28. 8:15 am
29. 8:57 am
30. 12.5 metres
31. 132
32. 18 750 kms
33. 48 000 kms
34. Mal and Badge
35. 720 m
36. Half the time
37. (a) 9; (b) 44
38. $244.35

MISCELLANEOUS AND SPECIALS

39. 30 cm
40. 19
41. 2,3,5,7,11,13
42. 1+3+6+........55=220
43. It must happen at least once per year; the maximum number of times in a year is 3
44. $2\sqrt{13}$
45. 60
46. 73
47. Natasha plays guitar; Leanne plays clarinet; Carmen plays drums
48. Digits were 7 and 6; the bill was $237.36
49. Terry: 5 half-filled, 1 full, 1 empty; Green Dog: 1 half-filled, 3 full, 3 empty; Slim: 1 half-filled, 3 full, 3 empty

    OR

    Terry: 3 half-filled, 2 full, 2 empty; Green Dog: 3 half-filled, 2 full, 2 empty;

    Slim: 1 half-filled, 3 full, 3 empty

50. 120 kms
51. 504
52. 10:20 PM
53. 1 200
54. 180
55. 6 750
56. 250 km
57. 6 women, 5 men and 3 children
58. $52.36
59. 4 x $1 notes; 1 x $5 note; 19 x $10 notes
60. 301 glasses
61. 1008
62. 27, 64, 125, 216
63. 40 days
64. 42
65. 133
66. Maria 3, Jose 7, Ernesto 37

Ω THE AUTHOR

JOHN CARTY has been

- A Senior Secondary Head mathematics Teacher for more than 30 years
- The director of the AST, the ACT Year 12 Senior scaling test for 15 years
- A Statistician in the manufacturing and health insurance industries for 6 years
- A tutor in Mathematics and Statistics for 20 years
- A member of the Problems' Committee of the Australian Mathematics Competition for 42 years.
- ACT Director of the Australian Mathematics Olympiad for 16 years

Ω
PROBLEM SOLVING STRATEGIES

We all use strategies to solve problems, most of us every day.

Why is it that only 20% of use could do those word-problems when we were in our teens? Each time we make a decision, we use one or more of the strategies listed below, even if it is only the one about exploring all possibilities. Let us apply some of those to mathematical word problems.

This is not an exhaustive list.

1. READ IT CAREFULLY – understand what the problem asks. Hurried Or careless reading is often the source of wrong answers.
2. RESTATE THE PROBLEM
3. GUESS AND CHECK OR TRIAL AND ERROR
4. MAKE A TABLE, CHART, set of lines group of boxes etc
5. DON'T RUSH
6. LOOK FOR PATTERNS
7. DON'T RUB OUT, cross-out lightly
8. DRAW A DIAGRAM, model or picture, tree-diagram
9. ELIMINATE POSSIBILITIES
10. WORK BACKWARDS
11. KEEP WRITING
12. ORGANISE DATA – have a good system of recording
13. USE LOGIC e.g. "what if"
14. ACT out a situation e.g. "stepping" with your feet or hands

MATHEMATICAL WORD PROBLEMS

15. SOLVE A SIMILAR SIMPLER PROBLEM
16. CUT OR FOLD UP PIECES OF PAPER
17. ESTIMATE
18. REMOVE EXTRNEIOUS INFORMATION. Some things may have nothing to do with the answer or solution.
19. IS IT AN EXTENSION OF A PROBLEM I have seen before?
20. CHECK LANGUAGE – Look for keywords e.g. successive, consecutive, less, Greater original, initial, if, unless, symmetrical, equal, double etc
21. UNITARY METHODS. Bring things to a basis of 1 e.g. "in one hour" "one cake needs", "one pointer will". This tactic is very useful in ratio, mixtures and rates questions.
22. IDENTIFY and CONQUER SUBTASKS and underline the solution to subtasks.
23. DON'T GIVE UP – GUESS AGAIN
24. IF A THOUGHT comes to you while doing something else – WRITE IT DOWN.
25. CHECK YOUR ANSWER – Read the question back with your answer in to see if it makes sense.
26. JUSTIF YOUR ANSWER
27. Completely STATE YOUR ANSWER. e.g. Don't just say "x=3" and stop. Instead say "Tom carried 3 cats upstairs".
28. WRITE DOWN A FEW STRATEGIES FOR FUTURE USE.
29. ALGEBRAIC TECHNIQUES

    This is what this book is about in one way – the great power of Algebra. You can solve systematically using Algebra – even if at times it is not the shortest solution. Now a few extra little strategies just for the parents who will tackle all 777 problems.

30. TAKE A FEW INTO WORK WITH YOU.
31. DON'T LOOK UP THE ANSWER at the back for 2-3 days at least.
32. DON'T push our children to use strategies they haven't mastered e.g. quadratic equations. In fact it may be counter-productive. This is a major problem with some senior curriculum designs.

www.ingramcontent.com/pod-product-compliance
Lightning Source LLC
Chambersburg PA
CBHW051348110526
44591CB00025B/2944